Unstoppable Heart

Dear Al,   May 31, 2019

Thank you for your interest, your warm heart and compassionate wisdom. Keep on keeping on

Ronnie Jordan

Unstoppable Heart

Ronnie Botwinick Londner

© 2016 Ronnie Botwinick Londner
All rights reserved.

ISBN: 0996939008
ISBN 13: 9780996939003
Library of Congress Control Number: 2015917034
Sonnenschein Books, Miami, FL

Dedication

To My Beloved Boys

Michael Londner — Precious son. A brief candle, but, oh, such light, such warmth.

Leonard Botwinick — Cherished father, friend, and "Marine." Thank you for teaching me to look at the rose, not the thorn.

Mark Londner — My husband, my heart, and my companion. The only other who truly knew.

Heymann Steinhardt — My maternal grandfather, my hero, my strength. He was one of the very few who escaped en route to a Holocaust death camp. He taught me by courageous example to keep on keeping on.

Contents

	Introduction	xi
Chapter 1	Scrabble Scramble	1
Chapter 2	Bassinet Rumble	8
Chapter 3	Adjusting to the NICU	13
Chapter 4	Numbers Are for Groups	19
Chapter 5	More Than Just a Brain Bleed	21
Chapter 6	Coming Home at Last	25
Chapter 7	Pivoting in the Library	29
Chapter 8	Home-Day Party	33
Chapter 9	Let's Have Another Baby—Teddy	36
Chapter 10	"Cast a Wide Net": To Sue or Not	38
Chapter 11	The Birth of the IVH Parents Support Group and PBS: *Frontline* Comes to Visit	42
Chapter 12	Walk on By	49
Chapter 13	Finding a School for Mikey	52
Chapter 14	It's a Small World	59
Chapter 15	Support Groups	63
Chapter 16	Homegrown Research: Why Do Some IVH Babies Do Better Than Others?	68
Chapter 17	Twin Brothers, Separated by Two Years	71
Chapter 18	Barbarism	75
Chapter 19	Freckle Feet	83
Chapter 20	Drones Club	85

Chapter 21	Mark's Words: On Fatherhood	89
Chapter 22	Skin So Soft	93
Chapter 23	Mikey's Secret	97
Chapter 24	Mikey Tells Teddy Something Important	99
Chapter 25	Ear Infection	101
Chapter 26	Mikey's Funeral	106
Chapter 27	Dr. Freund's Reaction	109
Chapter 28	Reassuring Montessori Classmates	111
Chapter 29	A Prayer for Organ Donors	114
Chapter 30	Grief	117
Chapter 31	The Visit	124
Chapter 32	Corresponding with Organ Recipients	127
Chapter 33	Grief's Unveiling	132
Chapter 34	Smelling the Storm	136
Chapter 35	Fishing for Life	143
Chapter 36	Contact Thwarted	145
Chapter 37	Searching for the Heart-Family	148
Chapter 38	Direct Contact	156
Chapter 39	Learning More	158
Chapter 40	Working Out My Grief	161
Chapter 41	"Play Ball!"	166
Chapter 42	Sneaky Grandmother	169
Chapter 43	Mark Beats the Odds	172
Chapter 44	Rushing to Robin	175
Chapter 45	Cancer Ablaze	178
Chapter 46	Finding a Safe Space	182
Chapter 47	Ethical Will	186
Chapter 48	"Once in Love with Amy"	190
Chapter 49	Ted's Gift	192
Chapter 50	A Weekend of Funerals	194
Chapter 51	Daddy	197
Chapter 52	Messages from Mark	201

Chapter 53	Disk Crash	203
Chapter 54	Meeting Nick, My Heart-Son	208
Epilogue:	Heart Sounds	213
	Acknowledgements	217
	About the Author	221

Introduction

I WROTE THIS BOOK BECAUSE it fell on me. It started as a snowflake and ended as an avalanche.

When I want to understand or remember something, I tend to take notes or write about it. Writing gives me the paradoxical power of emotional distance and depth. I can plumb because I've climbed up the mountain and have a wider, clearer view. A photojournalist once told me that the camera lens between his eye and the horrors he witnessed while covering wars enabled him to take the ghastly pictures he did. "If I'd seen the carnage without the camera, I couldn't have borne it," he told me. "I couldn't have done my job."

This book tells the story of my family. It's not the whole story—who can ever tell that?—but it's a vital slice.

The action in *Unstoppable Heart* begins with a sudden gush of blood down my leg in the twenty-ninth week of pregnancy. From there I take you with me into the world of premature birth, surgery on unanesthetized infants, disability issues, the death of my son Michael, organ donation, choices about pursuing lawsuits, decisions about having more children, the impact that schools and religious and medical institutions have on families, ethical wills, and the illnesses and deaths of my husband and my father.

But this world also contains joy and laughter: mischievous toddlers conducting midnight toast parties; an exhilarating monorail ride upfront with the conductor at Disney World; an extraordinary, loving relationship between brothers; a dog who joined in the brothers' games; and a shimmering, shining love among and between parents, children, and siblings.

For the eight years Michael lived, he defined our family. The early struggle depicted in this memoir was whether Michael would live to leave the neonatal intensive care unit. The next step was how to teach—and learn from—our disabled child. He thrived for a time and then suddenly died. A later struggle was whether the interference of a hospital worker would disrupt our living link to our son—our correspondence with the mother whose son received Michael's donated heart. The final struggle was to find and meet the recipient, to hear Michael's heart beat once more, and to embrace this young man, my heart-son, and his child, my heart-granddaughter, who live because Mikey died.

My story is particular to me, my family, and my circle. How those events occurred and how they were perceived and acted upon are unique to me. But my microcosm is within the macrocosm we all share—that larger circle that encompasses us all. As humanistic psychologist Carl Rogers said, "What is most personal is most universal."

All of us have had loss and sorrow as well as joy and delight. We lean on and learn from each other, wiping each other's tears and sharing blessed laughter. Remember the times you and another laughed so hard you had to prop each other up? What a glorious feeling it is to be "helpless" with laughter. We must persist through the bad times, but let's perpetuate the good times by ruminating happiness instead of sorrows or grudges.

Yes, we take a terrible chance when we love; but if we don't love, we don't live.

CHAPTER 1

Scrabble Scramble

There were so many turning points, so many places where we could have prevented Michael's life. The decision to do so would have stripped us of our most tremendous joys and our greatest griefs, but it would also have blocked the lives of an entire family that now exists because of him. The splash of Michael's life has ripples still vigorously spreading.

I've got some explaining to do.

We already had one child, a daughter, born in late 1977. I was a freelance writer for the *Miami Herald* and a few magazines, and Mark was a news reporter for WSVN, a local Miami television station. Our life was pleasant and smooth.

I remember the three of us—Mark, little Robin, and me—dancing in the living room one afternoon when Robin was two-and a-half-years old. I held Robin, and Mark held me as we spun and laughed to the music; I think it was something from *Sesame Street*.

"I am so happy!" I thought, reveling in the conscious joy of the moment. I had a husband I loved and respected; a bright, affectionate child; and many pleasant middle-class accouterments. But we, especially I, wanted at least one more child.

"We should be talking about having another baby, don't you think?" I asked my husband as we three hugged and twirled to the music.

"We are good as we are," Mark said.

"Oh yes, we are," I agreed, "but another baby would balance us, especially a boy, like the two-parent, one-girl, one-boy family I grew up in."

Mark stroked my cheek, and Robin put her face forward to him.

"Me too!" she demanded.

We both laughed, and Mark patted her little cheek too. He looked back at me and said, "We'll see."

When Robin was three, I got pregnant again. My first visit to the obstetrician went well. But about nine weeks into the pregnancy, I had some spotting. When Dr. Hanft examined me, he was sad. He was a kind man who told long, terrible jokes and loved his patients. He held my hand as he spoke and reached back to grasp Mark's hand too.

"You are dilated, and I think you'll miscarry in a day or two," he told us. "I should probably do a dilatation and curettage on you and abort the pregnancy now."

I felt squeezed and sad. Mark reached out to hold my hand, completing the circle. I asked if anything could be done to prevent the miscarriage.

"No, I don't think so," said Dr. Hanft. "But if you like, I won't do the D and C now, and we'll see what happens over the next few days. I doubt you'll keep the baby, but we can wait and see."

Later, I'd remember that moment for the crossroads it was. Mark and I looked at each other and silently made our decision via what we called marital mind meld.

"We'll go home and wait," said Mark as I nodded at Dr. Hanft.

That evening the bleeding stopped, and when I returned the next week, Dr. Hanft was surprised.

"You're not dilated at all anymore," he said after he examined me. "It's amazing."

Mark and I beamed at each other.

My pregnancy progressed without any further problems. I had a sonogram, and it showed a normally proportioned baby with a strong heartbeat. I loved listening to that sturdy, rapid heart. I felt well, happy, and full of anticipation. The baby was due mid-December 1981. The topic most in my thoughts was the method of birth. I hoped I could have a vaginal birth. When Robin was born, I'd had a Caesarean section after a long labor, which upset and disappointed me. Dr. Hanft was one of the first doctors in our area who helped women to have vaginal births after a Caesarean.

One evening in late September, Mark and I were playing Scrabble on our newly purchased waterbed. I was winning, but not by much. Robin "helped" me by rearranging the tiles on my rack. I felt the baby dart about inside me. I stroked my belly, trying to put my hand where I thought the baby's head was. With my other hand, I touched Robin's cheek and pushed a wild strand of her blond hair behind her ear. I was content as only a happily pregnant woman can be. Making my bliss complete, I finished the game by making a seven-letter word. Mark put the letter tiles away as I heaved my almost seven-months-pregnant body up off the bed.

"Good game, Mark. I'm going to take a shower," I told him, walking into the bathroom. But before I could begin to undress, I felt a gush. There was no pain, but a stream of blood began running down my leg onto the tile floor.

"Mark," I shouted, "call Dr. Hanft!"

On the rainy ride to the hospital to meet Dr. Hanft, I repeated to myself, "I'm having a miscarriage. My baby will die." I was trying to prepare for the loss of this longed-for child. But through my fears, the baby kicked and moved reassuringly. So, I tried to make my mind blank. I concentrated on calming my daughter and husband. I held Mark's hand, and I smiled at Robin, sleepily sitting in her car seat in the back. I adjusted the towel I was sitting on and checked for more blood. The gush had turned to an ooze. I stretched my hand out to the backseat and touched Robin's little hand. Then I faced forward again and looked out the window at the palm trees waving gently in the wet Miami night.

At the hospital, my friend Suzi met us to take Robin to her house for the night. Suzi stared at my bloodstained dress. She kissed me as she took Robin from my arms. That kiss was a good-bye to the old me and my old, pre-grief life.

Mark and I filled out the paperwork to admit me to the hospital. Name: Ronnie Londner. Today's date: September 27, 1981. Symptoms: Vaginal bleeding at twenty-eight weeks, five days gestation.

Dr. Hanft quickly diagnosed the problem: *placenta abruptio*, a tearing away of a normal placenta from the uterine wall. He told me to lie flat on my back. He hoped the placental tear might be small enough to allow the pregnancy to proceed for at least a few more weeks.

No one in my extended family had given birth prematurely. Robin had been born by Caesarean section four days past her due date. I had no idea what to expect.

For two-and-a-half days, I lay in a hospital bed, trying to heal. "Stay, stay," I begged the baby.

But then, three nights after the Scrabble game, a pain like hot needles tore through my womb. I began having contractions. Over and over, Dr. Hanft and the nurses felt my belly. Finally, after consulting with a pediatrician, Dr. Hanft told Mark and me, "We've got to do a Caesarean section. If we don't, the blood from the abruption will continue to back up behind the uterus. Ronnie, you could go into shock, and then you and the baby could die. The baby's chances for survival are not good now, but that's all we've got."

I lay still. Other people bustled about, preparing for the C-section. A nurse motioned toward my neck and said, "That jewelry needs to go, Mrs. Londner." Mark unhooked the teddy bear necklace I always wore. He put it in his pocket.

"Mr. Londner, you need to leave now," a nurse said. "Husbands aren't allowed once we start the surgery."

Mark's mouth formed an *O* of protest.

"He's staying here," Dr. Hanft bellowed. "I don't care about the policy—I care about this family."

The nurse rolled her eyes but nodded at Mark, who immediately went to my side and held my hand. "That's a first," she said. "We don't let fathers stay for Caesareans. But don't you get in the way or faint. If you do, you're out of here, despite what he says."

She glanced at Dr. Hanft, but he wasn't looking at her. He was talking rapidly to a newly arrived man in scrubs. The man told Hanft, "I got it; let's go," and moved over to me.

"I'm the anesthesiologist," he said as he and a nurse positioned me onto my side. "I'm going to give you a spinal block. No time for a pre-injection numbing first, sorry."

I felt the sting of a needle in my lower back. Then, my belly and legs seemed to disappear from my body. I was rolled to my back again, and I looked up to find Mark trying to smile at me.

We said simultaneously, "It'll be okay," and then we both smiled for real. A screen was propped over my belly to obscure my view of the surgery.

Dr. Hanft announced, "Here we go." Mark squeezed my hand. The screen was not well placed. I saw Dr. Hanft make the first incision. It looked like he was drawing a red line on my belly. I looked back into Mark's eyes and tried to smile again. Someone straightened the screen, and I couldn't see my belly anymore.

Through a fog of stress, I heard the voices of the nurses and doctors.

"It's a boy, small!" exclaimed Dr. Hanft as a tiny, angry cry filled the operating room.

I heard Mark gasp.

"APGAR: seven!" said pediatrician Alvin Freund, using the scoring method used to measure a newborn's health. "Two pounds, fifteen ounces, not bad," said another voice.

The baby was brought to me. I got an impression of pink, skinny sweetness. Then he was whisked away.

"APGAR improving, now eight," came the pediatrician's voice. "He looks good for a preemie."

Mark let go of my hand and kissed my forehead. He ran to follow our new son out of the operating room to where the transport team from the local children's hospital was waiting to take our baby to the neonatal intensive care unit (NICU). We had chosen the baby's first name, Michael, to honor Mark's father, who had passed away when Mark was a teenager.

My husband and new son were now both gone. Dr. Hanft continued to work on me, sewing my uterus and belly back together. After ten minutes, Dr. Hanft declared me ready for the recovery room. I was transferred to a gurney, but as the nurse began to steer me out the door, Dr. Hanft stopped her and came over to me. He held my hand for a long moment and then kissed it. It was old-fashioned, European, and thoroughly endearing.

"Try not to worry about your baby. I'll come check on you soon," he told me as he released my hand and allowed the nurse to proceed.

As the nurse trundled me down the hallway, we approached an open area where I saw a circle of people in scrubs surrounding what appeared to be medical equipment. I just knew my son had to be at the center.

"Oh, please stop!" I begged the nurse. She took me closer to the hubbub of activity surrounding my micro-infant and told me, "Just for a moment. We've got to get you to recovery."

Michael was lying on a miniature version of the gurney I was on. The transport technicians and doctors were placing plastic adhesive patches on his chest and legs. An angel-hair-sized intravenous line was already flowing into his foot. He was wearing a tiny ski cap–type hat.

I propped myself up on one elbow and asked the nearest person in blue scrubs, "May I touch him?" The man nodded and said, "Be quick. We have to move your baby to the incubator now to preserve his energy and body heat while we transport him to the children's hospital."

The nurse steered me in even closer. I stretched my hand as far as I could. My straining fingers found Michael's soft, cool cheek. His eyes were tightly closed, as though he couldn't bear to see the world yet.

"Oh, my Mikey, I'm sorry," I said.

The man in blue told me, "We have to take him now. The ambulance is waiting. Your husband is already outside; he'll ride with us."

He placed Mikey into the portable incubator, gently arranging the wires and tubes. He glanced back over his shoulder and said to me, "We'll take good care of him." Then he and the other transport team members walked rapidly away, wheeling the incubator in front of them.

I thought of Mikey's life as it had been until a half-hour ago. He had been swimming in my uterus with no need to breathe or see, hearing soothing sounds, just floating and growing. When the placenta that had sustained him tore, my womb transformed from a haven into a hazard, and he was ripped from my body to save his life. But now he was plugged into a Plexiglas medical box being rushed down a hallway by strangers.

The nurse began pushing my gurney again, on track to the recovery room. I lay back as she hustled down the hallway. I still couldn't feel my legs, but my chest felt tight. I lifted my hand and looked at the fingers that had touched Mikey's face. I put them to my mouth and kissed them. Then I, too, tightly closed my eyes.

CHAPTER 2

Bassinet Rumble

I HAD A PRIVATE ROOM on the maternity floor. It had been two days since Michael had been taken from me. Every few hours, the bassinets would rumble by, headed for mothers who gave birth after nine months, not six-and-a-half. But Mark and I tried to keep cheerful and hopeful. Every day Michael lived, we thought, was a day closer to a joyous homecoming.

The neonatologists at the hospital where Michael had been sent told us our son had trouble breathing and had been put on a respirator. This was common for preemies, Mark and I were told, so the news didn't unduly alarm us. Friends and relatives who visited me at the hospital said things like, "Oh, if you have to have a premature baby, it's lucky you had him now when neonatology is so advanced. He'll be fine." Their Pollyanna reassurance was meant to comfort themselves as much as me. It didn't work, at least not on me.

I would smile and stroke the place where my pregnant belly had been. When I felt a gas pain or the pull of a Caesarean stitch, I'd think for an instant that the baby was kicking. Then I would remember where baby Michael was.

"I feel like I haven't given birth," I told Mark. "I feel like I've had an amputation."

Mark felt torn apart, too. While I was in South Miami Hospital, Mark would put in a long work day as a television news reporter and then visit me in one hospital and Mikey in the other. We both worried that our daughter, Robin, was getting lost in the collapse of our normal family life. We were grateful my parents had come down from New York to stay in our house and care for her.

When Mark arrived at the NICU each evening, he washed his hands vigorously for the three mandatory minutes. Next he pulled the required sterile yellow gown over his street clothes. He could then approach Mikey's warmer. Standing, Mark talked to Michael, stroking his back or shoulder or whatever part of his tiny body he could reach. When Mark touched Mikey's hand, Mikey's micro-fingers grasped Mark's thick pinkie finger.

On days that Mikey was stable, Mark sat in a rocking chair as a nurse carefully arranged the baby's wires and tubes so she could hand the tiny boy to his eager father. Mark told me the love, sorrow, and protective feelings that welled up inside made him lightheaded with longing.

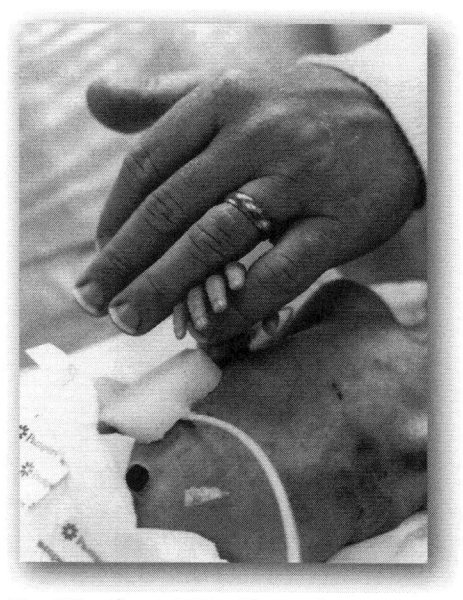

I was still in South Miami Hospital. Dr. Hanft and Dr. Freund came to visit me often. Dr. Hanft said there was no known reason for my placental abruption. It's rare, occurring in about one in five hundred pregnancies, he said, explaining the fetal mortality rate was close to 50 percent.

One morning, Dr. Freund came into my hospital room. A nurse was helping me get out of bed, but Dr. Freund asked her to leave. His face was tight and gray. My heart began to pound as I sank back onto the bed. The nurse touched my shoulder gently and left the room. It was Michael's fourth day of life.

Dr. Freund said, "This is bad. We think Michael had a massive brain hemorrhage last night."

I looked hard at the top of Dr. Freund's head. I felt sweat beading in the small of my back.

"He's still alive, but it doesn't look good." Dr. Freund looked at my bed tray, at the chair, at anything but my face.

"What do you mean, you think he had a brain hemorrhage?" I gasped. I had trouble inhaling enough air to speak.

"It'll be confirmed by ultrasound one way or another, but it's pretty clear to me," answered Dr. Freund. "His hematocrit dropped several points suddenly last night, and the most likely place for the blood to go is the ventricles of the brain." Still not looking at me, he said, "I'm sorry," and he left the room.

Holding my breath, I reached for the phone. It was hard to push the buttons with a shaking hand. I called my husband at work.

"Mark," I gasped, "Dr. Freund just told me that Michael has had a—a brain hemorrhage." I started to sob in an ugly way. "Please come to me!"

Mark was soon at my side. The nurses left us alone to cry. Our pain was primitive and unrelenting. We held each other, wordlessly.

After a time, Mark released our embrace and stood up.

"I need to go to see Mikey, and find a doctor to explain this to me. Okay?" he asked.

"Of course," I told him. "Maybe it isn't so bad as all that. Call me as soon as you can."

Mark smiled sadly at me and left. Later, he told me that when he got to the children's hospital he sought out the pediatric neurologist, who confirmed the diagnosis: a grade IV intraventricular hemorrhage (IVH). It is not uncommon in preemies, the doctor said, and is a leading cause of death and disability.

Standing together at Mikey's incubator, the pediatric neurologist explained the grading system of bleeds to Mark. Grade I bleeds occur in the germinal matrix, an area of the brain active during fetal development that disappears about five weeks before the baby's due date. Grade II bleeds extend beyond grade I to the brain's ventricles but don't involve enlargement of the ventricles. Ventricles are interconnected cavities in the brain where cerebrospinal fluid is made. Grade III bleeds go beyond grade II to include enlargement of the ventricles from accumulated blood. Grade IV bleeds go beyond grade III to bleeding that extends into brain tissue around the ventricles.

Grades I and II are most common, the doctor explained, and often there are no further complications. Grades III and IV, however, may result in long-term brain injury to the infant. And our baby had a grade IV bleed—the worst.

The doctor was gentle, kind, and sad as he explained the grading system, Mark told me later. He also said he had to hold his breath a few times while the doctor was speaking so he wouldn't burst into tears.

That evening, alone in my hospital room, I tried not to listen to the rumble of baby bassinets going past my door. One set of rolling wheels got especially loud. I looked up as a smiling nurse I hadn't seen before pushed a bassinet right up to my bed.

"Here's your baby, all ready to nurse!" she said brightly.

For an instant I thought, "It's all a dream; Michael is healthy." Then I realized the ludicrous, tormenting mistake.

"My baby is at the children's hospital," I told the nurse, and I turned away.

I heard a quiet, shocked "Oh, I'm sorry."

The wheels rattled away to the new mother waiting in the room next door. When the other nurses learned of the mistake, one came to give me an extra pain shot and held my hand while it took effect.

"There's all kinds of pain," she told me.

Early the next morning, when I awoke from that drug-induced sleep, Dr. Hanft was standing next to my bed. He was looking at my Polaroid photo of Mikey. Two days earlier a thoughtful nurse at the children's hospital gave the photo to Mark for me. Hanft turned when he realized I was awake. He touched my shoulder and said, "I know you need to see your baby. I'm releasing you from the hospital earlier than usual. Being with Mikey will be better medicine than any I can give you."

When Mark came to pick me up, he brought my maternity jeans, a soft gray sweatshirt, and my teddy bear necklace. We left South Miami Hospital empty-handed and full of grief.

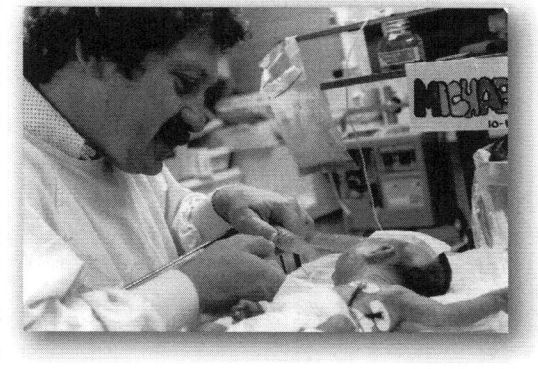

We drove directly to the children's hospital. Someone brought a wheelchair, and I was taken upstairs to the neonatal intensive care unit. Shaking and light-headed from weakness, I leaned against the sink and scrubbed carefully for the requisite three minutes. I then put on the yellow hospital gown and walked in to see my five-day-old baby.

The incessant noise of monitors beeping, harsh lighting (the better to observe the babies' conditions), and strong odors of disinfectant and plastic assailed me. I saw busy doctors, nurses, and technicians standing over the

Isolettes (high tech versions of bassinettes) treating each tiny patient and hurrying on to the next. Some family members stood as I did, frozen. Perhaps they, too, were new here. Parents who seemed more familiar with the lights, sounds, and smells sat next to the bassinets and talked or sang to their babies.

Pink and blue teddy bears decorated the walls and a colorful, hand-drawn sign with each baby's name was taped to each bassinet.

"Where is he?" I asked Mark, who stood next to me. He was familiar with the unit and pointed to the center of the room. In the middle of the third row was a bassinet with a card on it: MICHAEL.

Mark asked, "Shall I come with you?"

"No, not this time," I answered. "Do you understand?"

"Not really," he answered, smiling slightly. "But I don't have to. Do what you need to do."

With fear and eagerness, I walked alone to my son.

I gazed down at Michael in his bassinet warmer. He was too sick and tiny even for an Isolette. The words *beautiful, tiny, blighted, suffering, mine* ran through my mind as I stared at my son. His chest heaved with each click of the respirator. Intravenous lines and monitor wires ran over the tiny body that should have still been floating peacefully in my womb.

I focused on Michael's tiny hand. "May I touch him?" I asked the nurse. At her nod, I picked up the little hand and kissed it. "Hello, Michael," I said. "It's Mama."

As I spoke to my baby, I saw the nurse squint, surprised, at one of the monitors.

"His pO_2 level is climbing—look!" she said.

The monitor numbers went from 82 to 84, 86, 88, 92, and beyond.

"The higher the pO_2 level, the better he is using his oxygen," the nurse explained. "That's a direct result of him feeling better. It's hearing your voice that did it. It may sound different from this side of the uterus, but he knows his mother!"

She grabbed a pen and Mikey's chart and wrote busily for a moment. When she looked up, she was smiling at me. She turned the chart around and placed it in my tentatively outstretched hand. I read, "pO_2 levels ☒ 82 to 95 when mother spoke to patient." I returned the chart and the smile.

My son and I had communicated.

CHAPTER 3

Adjusting to the NICU

I NEARLY HAD TO BE thrown out of the NICU that first day. Though I was wobbly with weakness and overwhelmed by the lights, noises, and smells of the unit, I didn't want to leave my baby. I leaned on Mikey's warmer, too weak to continue standing for long. Mark helped me back into the wheelchair as I repeatedly told my son, "I'll be back. I love you. Mama loves you." An aide pushed me to the elevator as Mark held my hand and walked beside me. On the way home in the car, I cried so violently that it felt like my tear ducts were heaving. Mark held my hand as he drove, and I saw tears running down his face. My stomach churned and my head ached. I was Mikey's mother—I should have protected him, I thought. The doctors had assured me again and again that these things happened and that I had done nothing to cause the placenta abruptio. It was a brief comfort, but as I thought of what Mikey was enduring, my need to be near him, to touch him, drowned me again.

Privacy became a rare commodity for Mark and me. We could talk in the car and in bed at night before we both fell into a restless doze. My parents were staying on with us and were an enormous help. But as we wished to spare them as much of our anguish and worry as we could, their presence was, at times, inhibiting.

There was no privacy in the NICU. The unit didn't have cubicles; it needed to be open so the medical people had immediate access. On rare occasions a portable screen was placed around the "bedside." But that scrap of privacy usually indicated trouble; a baby was getting a procedure, receiving CPR, or worse. We parents looked at each other fearfully when the screen was dragged around. Was the baby on the other side dying? Sometimes, the answer was yes.

From behind the screen, we often heard the voices of doctors and nurses. They ranged from strident to soothing. The occasional sob could be heard afterward from mothers, grandmothers, and more than a few fathers. Another hint to a family's condition was whether a baby was stable enough for a loved one to find a way through the tangle of IVs and wires to stroke the child's chest or legs with a gentle finger. A hand would be too large. If a baby was doing very well, a nurse might carefully lift the infant out of the Isolette to be held by a grateful, and often terrified, parent.

The relationships of NICU parents with each other were complex. Most of us wanted to give each other privacy. But we also wanted to know these strangers who likely understood more about what we were going through than did our closest family and friends. I'd look up from Mikey's bassinet sometimes and catch the eye of a mother a few feet away. We'd both quickly look away, awkwardly. It was like being in traffic and idly looking over at the car in the next lane, only to be startled to see the other driver staring back.

One day when the mother parked next to me caught my glance yet again, we smiled at each other. Then we moved our chairs closer and introduced ourselves by telling each other our babies' names and gestational ages at birth. Eventually, we got to our own names. Olga, whose son was born at thirty-and-a-half-weeks gestation—a whole ten days further along than Mikey—was my alter ego in many respects. She wore makeup. Her hair and nails were perfect. She was beautifully dressed, down to her red high heels.

"Olga, how do you do it? You look so good," I said, rubbing my nail-bitten hands on my sweat pants. I tried to be jealous, but I was too tired.

"Oh, it's very important to look right," she told me. "You have to show respect."

"Respect to whom?" I asked her.

"To the doctors," she replied. She lowered her voice so much I had to lean in to hear her. She looked around before answering. "They have much power."

I was puzzled and wanted to ask her to explain, but a nurse came to her baby's bassinet, and Olga's attention to our conversation was gone.

I went to the NICU every day, sometimes with Mark and other times with one of my parents. Sometimes I saw Olga there, and sometimes I didn't.

With my parents in residence, there was a new family dynamic. In addition to driving me as I recovered from surgery, my parents took Robin to and from preschool. They also shopped, cooked, and helped with household chores.

I felt guilty for crying so much in front of Robin, now nearly four years old. My delightful little girl—beautiful, clever, funny, fastidious, and highly intelligent—had been the princess of our extended family. She was the first grandchild in Mark's family of Holocaust survivors and the first granddaughter in my family of mostly European refugees and immigrants. She had been the center of attention at family gatherings, all eyes and ears on her. Everyone had plenty of time for her and interest in what she had to say. Now she saw grown-ups with frowns and tears, rushing to and from hospitals. Her world toppled with her brother's birth.

"What can we do for her?" Mark asked me.

"I don't know," I responded. "This is so unfair to Robin."

"This is so unfair to all of us," he said.

Mark and I had many talks with neurologists and neonatologists. Although Michael's prognosis for survival was poor, each day he stayed alive his chances improved. But what kind of life would it be? At what point do we say, enough already, let this poor child be? Dr. Freund had the same questions.

Mark and I had heard of profoundly disabled babies being subjected to agonizing treatments by medical professionals. These doctors were often eager to break new ground by keeping even the tiniest, most damaged neonates alive. And parents who wished to opt for compassionate care to allow a peaceful death for their infant were often vilified.

Mark had a chance to think about these things as he commuted back and forth to work. He told me his thoughts in the middle of yet another night when neither of us could sleep.

"I see facets of abortion, torture, compassion, end-of-life care, rights of people with disabilities, and parental responsibilities," he said. "Is Mikey being tortured to life?"

"And what kind of life?" I replied as I alternately flattened and plumped my pillow. I heard Mark sigh as he turned over to try to sleep.

We gathered what facts and opinions we could on Mikey's prognosis. It was sometimes hard to know where to start, what questions to ask. At that time, all the NICU doctors except one predicted moderate to severe mental retardation and physical disability if Mikey survived. A few physicians told us, off the record, that if Mikey was their baby they would allow him to die in peace. But the one exception, a pediatric neurologist, continued to give us a much cheerier forecast. During one of the conferences we had with him in his office, he waved studies at us that he said included prognoses of only mild to moderate disabilities. He put the papers on his desk and, when I leaned over to read the articles, he flipped them over. I had gotten the merest glimpse of two of the titles. I asked to see the studies, and while he promised to give me copies, he never did. Finally, I visited the hospital's medical library and used its microfilm collection to look up the two articles whose titles I had seen. I found what the doctor was hiding from us—those studies included children with much less severe hemorrhages than my child had had. They were not relevant to Michael. I slammed the microfilm back into its canister. I never again trusted that doctor.

The next time my hospital visit coincided with Olga's was on a day I got bad news about Mikey's latest follow-up brain scan. The pediatric neurologist stood with me next to Mikey's bassinet, showing me test results. He glanced at the papers in his hand and told me, "The brain damage is quite extensive. If he survives, his chances for any kind of normal life are suboptimal."

I looked at my beautiful son and felt breathless, drowning in the terrible words coming from the doctor. Out of the corner of my eye, I saw Olga look up at me, sympathy in her expressive face.

"Doctor, can we please go into an office or at least move across the room to discuss this?" I asked him.

"What? No, why? We can talk here," he answered, rattling the papers.

"I don't want to talk about this in front of Michael," I replied. "It's not respectful."

He looked at me like I was the one who needed a brain scan. "He doesn't know what I am saying," the doctor replied. He was impatient and annoyed, probably at being delayed by me for what seemed a nonsensical reason. I was getting annoyed too, and it showed.

"You may well be correct that he doesn't understand the words, but all the same I don't think it's right to assume he is unaware of the negative feelings those words convey," I said angrily. "We can move a few feet to discuss this."

"Oh, all right," said the doctor, grudgingly complying with my wish.

As I walked across the unit with the doctor, I saw Olga staring at me, horrified.

When the doctor finished, I walked back to Mikey's bassinet and stroked his leg through my tears. I felt a soft hand on my shoulder and turned to see Olga next to me.

I was sure she had come to comfort me about the bad report. But she looked at me sternly and said, "Oh, my friend, you must not do that!"

"Do what?" I asked.

"Be so fresh with the doctor. Remember their power," she replied.

"What do you mean? What power?" I asked, suddenly remembering Olga had mentioned power before, but I hadn't understood what she meant.

Olga whispered to me. "They hate the mothers to speak up or ask too many questions. How do you know they won't get angry with you and do something bad to your baby when you go home later?"

I was stunned. I struggled for words as Olga's perfectly groomed eyebrows squeezed together as she frowned at me. "Oh, Olga, no, I don't believe that for a minute. Some of these doctors may be poor communicators and somewhat insensitive, but they would never take out their annoyance with me on my baby."

Sadly, she shook her head at me, convinced I was naïve.

"You never know," she said. "Better to play the game. Be what they want."

I was no longer impressed with Olga's perfection anymore. She lived in worse fear than did I. I gave Olga a halfhearted hug and walked back to Mikey.

That night I spoke to Mark about the "suboptimal" findings of the latest brain scan. Then I made an appointment for us to talk with the head of neonatology about the implications and choices to be made. We felt comfortable with her on the many occasions she stopped by to check on Mikey and talk with us. She seemed kind, and I believed we had a rapport with her.

"She'll listen and help us sort out this terrible choice," Mark said to me as we trudged through the hospital hallways to the NICU the morning of our appointment.

We arrived at her office, and she stood to greet us. After we all sat down and we introduced the topic, Mark said, "The statistics are horrible for our little boy. The studies indicate what many of the doctors here tell us—that the likelihood is Mikey will have a short life filled with pain."

"While we aren't saying we want to stop treatment, we want to know what would happen if we did," I added.

"We would sue you to continue Michael's treatment," she replied. Her face changed from benign to belligerent.

Mark and I exchanged glances of shock and disappointment. The "we're in this together" feeling we previously had with this doctor evaporated. She heard a legal question, not our heartfelt concern about his prognosis and well-being.

Maybe if we'd asked Al Freund, a fellow physician, to accompany us, she would have been more receptive to our question and better able to hear what we were asking. Maybe not. As it was, we stayed a few more minutes and then left her office to stand by Mikey's warmer and hold each other's hand.

CHAPTER 4

Numbers Are for Groups

SOME OF THE DOCTORS WERE brusque when giving bad news. One of the neurologists would not make eye contact with me; the closest he got was to glare at my left ear while rattling off his news: "Likely prognosis is severe to moderate mental retardation and severe to moderate spasticity as sequelae to grade four intraventricular hemorrhage." I knew this apparent insensitivity was born of awkwardness, not coldness. It's hard to give bad news.

That made Dr. Richard Wilker, one of Mikey's neonatologists, all the more unusual when he took me into his tiny office one afternoon to explain some new test results. Dr. Wilker and I sat down. He stared at a photo on his desk of his wife and baby daughter. Then he looked me in the eye. He leaned forward and touched my hand for a moment. He sat back and began to speak, stumbling over his words at first.

"Well, uh, there is, apparently, uh, results indicate…there appears to be a great deal of damage. I'm so sorry. I wish we could prevent these things."

I was wearing the yellow surgical gown over my clothes. I slumped in the hard plastic chair, my legs stretched out in front of me.

19

I looked down and noticed without caring that my legs were stubbly with black hair.

"Blighted," I thought as Dr. Wilker continued to talk, citing statistics. "My beautiful boy is blighted."

Dr. Wilker droned on, but as he spoke his tone became firmer, more sure.

"But numbers are for groups. Your baby is an individual, and who knows how much of a recovery he can make with your help. Genetics help, too."

His words made me think of the strong and clever people in my family. My grandfather, Heymann Steinhardt, escaped while being transported to a concentration camp in Nazi Germany. My great-grandfather, Michael Steinhardt, could pick up a cow and walk across the barnyard with her. My cousin, Mikhail Botvinnik, was a chess grand master during the 1950s. My uncle Walter used to insist we are related to Albert Einstein.

I sat up straight, tucked my feet under me, and mentally saluted my forebears. Two of those relatives were also named Michael, I thought. We picked a good name. I smiled at Dr. Wilker. "You're right, of course. Thank you for reminding me."

I decided to shave my legs when I got home. I didn't need to be a perfectly groomed Olga, but I did need to be myself if I was going to help my child. The next day, I brought Robin to the NICU for the first time.

"This is your brother," I told her as she stood on a stepstool to be able to see Mikey, crisscrossed with wires, in his bassinette. "This is our family now."

CHAPTER 5

More Than Just a Brain Bleed

MICHAEL HAD PROBLEMS BEYOND THE brain hemorrhage. His heart would beat so fast and hard that I could see it pounding in his thin chest. This was caused by patent ductus arteriosus, a condition fairly common in premature babies. The ductus arteriosus connects the pulmonary artery and aorta during fetal life and normally closes soon after birth in a full-term baby. In a premature baby, the ductus often remains open, or patent, causing the heart to overwork. A patent ductus can lead to an enlarged heart, heart failure, brain damage, and death. Sometimes a drug (indomethacin) can be used to close the ductus. Michael's was too large, so a surgical ligation was done. The heart operation was successful, and Michael's overworked, enlarged heart calmed and shrank to proper size.

Next, Michael developed pneumonia. The doctors thought he would go into a coma and die. He didn't. He got better. He was five weeks old and still so small, a little more than two pounds, down about ten ounces from his birth weight of two pounds, fifteen ounces.

Mikey improved enough to be able to breathe sometimes without a respirator. The doctors would take him off, and a few hours later his blood gases showed he couldn't make it on his own. He would go back on the respirator, increasing his chances for permanent lung damage.

Around this time, the soft spot (anterior fontanelle) on Michael's skull grew tense. His head circumference was measured often, and the doctors pursed their lips and shook their heads when they read the measurements. The veins in Michael's forehead became taut and shiny.

We were told he had hydrocephalus as a result of the brain hemorrhage. A doctor explained that spinal fluid is normally present in the ventricles, or cavities, of the brain. Ordinarily, new fluid is made and absorbed in the ventricles. But Michael's hemorrhage, which occurred in a ventricle, upset the balance, and now spinal fluid was not being reabsorbed. It was building up and pressing against the brain, causing the fontanelle to bulge. Sometimes hydrocephalus gets better spontaneously, but, for Mikey, it didn't.

Many spinal taps were made in hopes of relieving the pressure, but they proved useless. Then, a ventriculostomy was performed. A needle was inserted through Michael's skull and brain to the ventricles; excess fluid drained into a bag. The needle and bag can be left in place for no longer than five days, for fear of infection.

On the third day, Mikey's ventriculostomy "exploded."

Doctors disagreed on whether this latest insult, as these medical disasters are called, caused more brain damage. The visible result was a tiny baby with a shrunken head. So much spinal fluid leaked out during the night before the accident was discovered at the end of a sixteen-hour nursing shift that Mikey's skull collapsed on itself. Now Michael had too little spinal fluid.

Michael suffered greatly over the next few days until the fluid built up again and returned to normal. The doctors acknowledged that Michael probably had a headache, but they said nothing could be done for him. Mark and I squirmed in our powerlessness to help him. Our emotional exhaustion became apparent when Mark said, "He needed that like a hole in the head," and we both laughed until we leaned against each other and sobbed.

We hoped the "explosion" had, at least, stopped the hydrocephalus, but the pressure built up again. After a ventricular tap (insertion of a needle, usually through the anterior fontanelle, to withdraw cerebrospinal fluid from the lateral ventricle) proved useless, a shunt was finally placed in Michael's head to permanently drain the excess fluid from the brain to the abdomen. A shunt is internal. The only thing visible from the outside is a bump on the skull.

The shunt worked. The hydrocephalus was controlled.

By then Michael had been in the hospital about nine weeks, and we were becoming used to the seesaw of horror and hope. One of my mother's friends asked for permission to pray that Michael would die. Mark and I wanted our son to be free from pain and capable of happiness. Should Michael suffer and live to spend his days twisted and remote from normal life? But we also wanted our son with us. Could all these wishes be granted?

Those days and weeks turned into months. Mark and I suffered, often in different ways. He had the difficulty and relief of living in another world for eight or nine hours a day, reporting the often-diverting happenings of South Florida for the viewers of WSVN news. I stayed home with Robin, my freelance writing for the *Miami Herald* and other publications at a standstill. I was emotionally underwater. On the surface, way above, I could see the rest of the world, happy or only temporarily sad. People up there seemed to me to be moving from emotion to emotion, while I felt cringing and curled up in a "what next?" fetal position. I reminded myself of Dr. Wilker's words: "Genetics help, too." But Mikey still lay there and suffered, while Mark and I suffered in our helplessness to aid him.

After the shunt operation, Michael came off the respirator and stayed off. When Mikey graduated from his feeding tube to take a bottle by mouth, Mark was the first to feed him. Mikey took breast milk and formula and was moved from intensive care to the progressive care unit. Unable to turn off his reporting nature, Mark wrote down his thoughts and then refined them into an article for a parent support group:

> After the usual ten-hour pressure cooker day at the office, I faced another hour of bumper-to-bumper traffic on I-95. Would my reward for enduring this aggravation be dinner and an easy chair? No. I was heading for the neonatal intensive care unit at Miami Children's Hospital.
>
> Night after night, I scrubbed with surgical soap, put on my yellow gown, and sat in a wooden rocking chair. Then the nurses handed me my infant son. I began to feed him, giving him the breast milk my wife had pumped and stored. It took him an eternity to take even an ounce from the tiny bottle I held. He could barely suck.

As I sat cradling my tiny baby, I thought: "This must be the bonding that women talk about." I was forced by circumstance to do the woman's work of feeding my newborn. I was connecting with him the way most fathers can't or won't.

Mikey continued to do well for another week. Then, suddenly, he began to have seizures.

I watched his now four-pound body jolt as the seizures struck again and again. Between bouts, the nurses permitted me to stroke and soothe him. The nurses suffered with us. Michael had become a favorite with many of the medical staff because of his tenacity. His nickname was Iron Mike. After two days, the seizures ceased. We didn't know what caused them, but, as usual, the doctors told us the seizures were "common in premature babies."

Next Michael developed double inguinal hernias, which required surgery. A pediatric ophthalmologist noted Mikey's retinas were crisscrossed with many small blood vessels that had the potential to blind him. Mark and I added "premature retina, grade III" to our worries.

Like many preemies, Michael had numerous episodes of slow heartbeat (bradycardia) and cessation of breathing (apnea). Michael turned blue and had to be slapped on the feet, jostled, or given oxygen to bring him around. But he slowly continued to improve as his body systems matured and became more sturdy. Mark and I began to believe Mikey would come home.

CHAPTER 6

Coming Home at Last

I HELD MY BREATH FOR a long moment the day Mikey was deemed stable enough to be unhooked from the heart monitor.

"How can his heart beat if we don't hear it?" I smiled as I asked the nurse who was disengaging the wires.

Mark and I, as well as Mikey's nurses and doctors, watched him carefully over the next few days. Then, after eighty days in the Miami Children's Hospital, Michael came home. It was December 19, 1981, the week he should have been born. It was also Mark's and my fifth wedding anniversary, but it became known as Mikey's Home-Day. We reckoned his age and counted his milestones from that date for his first three years.

Finally, at long last, I was sitting in the backseat of the family Chevrolet Caprice as a smiling nurse gently handed me my five-pound, two-ounce son to place in his car seat. Mark fidgeted in the driver's seat, peering at us anxiously in the rearview mirror. Mikey was wearing a soft-blue coming-home outfit my mother had bought in hopes this day would come. Ever since I knew I was pregnant, I'd looked forward to bringing my newborn home. But Mark and I had envisioned a healthy, nine-months-gestation infant, not this scary, tiny, brain-injured baby we loved so desperately.

The nurse watched as I carefully pulled Mikey's little arms through the car seat straps. I wanted the nurse to go away, to stop looking at me with what I perceived as pitying eyes. I also frantically wanted her to get in the car with us and never leave me to care for my baby alone.

Mikey slept that first night, and many more, in a cheerful yellow bassinette right up against my side of the bed. Those first days and nights, Mark and I propped ourselves up on our elbows and stared at Mikey for hours while he slept. I would put my hand on his chest—was it moving? I would look at his tiny nose to see the flutter of breath in his nostrils. I would gaze at the bump in his skull where the shunt was. What would his life be like? And ours?

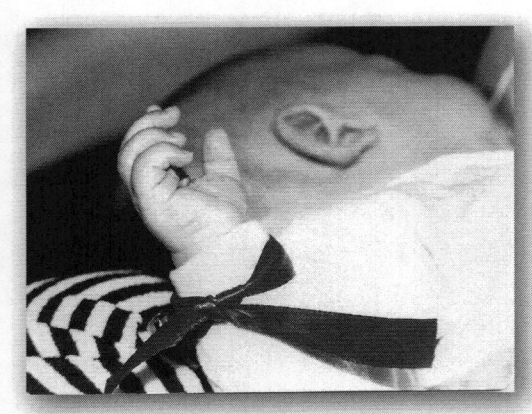

When Mark's mother, Hanni, came to see Mikey for the first time at home, she put a red ribbon (*bendele,* in Yiddish) on his right wrist.

"It's so the evil eye won't get him," she explained. Hanni was a sophisticated woman and didn't really believe in the power of a magic eye's malevolent gaze. But superstitions run deep and strong, and talismans in many cultures attempt to ward off the curse of the evil eye. As she tied the ribbon over the sleeve of her grandson's tiny yellow onesie, I thought of barn doors banging shut after many horses had already stampeded out. But I only smiled at Hanni and made no objection. After she went home that day, I started to take the *bendele* off but then shrugged my shoulders and left it on.

Dr. Wilker had said numbers were for groups and I could help Mikey in his individual recovery. I wanted to research that group to know what the range of possibilities might be with my individual. I needed to find other babies who had intraventricular hemorrhages. I wanted to see how they were doing. I asked doctors and nurses who were in touch with parents of survivors to contact me if they were willing. Several did so, and they knew others outside Miami. Soon I had a small group of parents in various cities throughout the country eager to talk to me and each other. Some children were reportedly doing fairly well, but the oldest was only five years old. Due to earlier lung maturation, girls often did better than boys and black children generally did better than white.

Mark and I knew it was vital for Michael to have any advantage we could give him. I knew breastfeeding was best, but during the eighty days Mikey was in the neonatal intensive care unit, my milk had dried up despite my continual pumping.

I had nursed Robin for two years, so I knew I could breastfeed. But now my breasts were dry. Dr. Freund told me that, with some work, it would be possible to get the breast milk back—to relactate. My mother went to the library for me to get me books on the topic. I read about adoptive mothers who had relactated and even about male lactation. I consulted with breastfeeding support group La Leche League and spoke often with Dr. Freund. He was helpful and encouraging.

I marshaled my resources: a plastic device called a Lact-Aid, recommended by La Leche League, and my friend Suzi's good-humored baby. A Lact-Aid is a bag worn between the breasts. From the bag runs a slim, flexible, straw-like tube that goes over a breast and ends at the nipple. The infant is placed at the breast and, though the breast is dry, the baby drinks the formula or donated breast milk from the bag. The baby's sucking, meanwhile, stimulates the breast to produce milk.

Suzi's little girl, Amy, was about six months older than Mikey. Suzi had plenty of milk. Amy, who had a head of red hair and a shining personality, was an avid nurser. We got together several times a week and switched babies—Suzi wet-nursed Mikey, and I dry-nursed Amy.

The first few times I nursed Amy, she latched on cheerfully enough, but after a few sucks she stopped, pulled away and looked up at me.

"Who are you, Dry Boob?" her expression said. "This isn't right."

But when I said, "It's okay, Amy, keep going," she went back to work and gave me a good five minutes on each side. She happily tugged on my teddy bear necklace while she suckled. Meantime, Mikey was at Suzi's breast drinking as fast as he could, sputtering and coughing in the cascade of milk.

We did this for several weeks until my breasts started to produce milk. Oh, happy day when I could finally nurse Mikey by myself. My tears and milk dripped in equal proportion. At last, I had a marvelous mammary munificence for Mikey.

In addition to breastfeeding at home, Mikey nursed in the waiting rooms at numerous doctors' offices. I spent hours every week taking Mikey to see medical people: neurologists, neurosurgeons, ophthalmologists, pediatricians, cardiologists, orthopedists, therapists, and early intervention specialists. I often had to take Robin with me. I kept a stash of toys and drawing materials for her in my baby bag, but they didn't always hold her attention for the long consultations.

When Mikey was home for about three months, we went to a new pediatric neurologist. Robin played with her toys on the floor while I talked to the doctor. He had a white plaster replica of the human spinal column placed on the corner of his desk.

After about fifteen minutes, Robin got bored with the baby doll she'd been amusing herself with. She looked around the room and noticed the model of the spine on the doctor's desk. She stood up, tippy-toed to her full height of three feet, and stretched her hand up to touch it. The doctor interrupted his discourse to me on brain plasticity in neonates to smile at Robin. His tone of voice morphed from pedantic to paternal.

"Those are backbones, sweetheart. We all have those."

Robin turned to me, excited. "Mama! Backbones! They look just like vertebrae!"

I shifted Mikey in my lap as I chortled at my brilliant daughter. The doctor grinned and said, "Well, I guess I can't patronize her. Let's hope that level of intelligence runs in the family."

I kissed the top of Mikey's head, willing that it was so.

CHAPTER 7

Pivoting in the Library

I HELD MIKEY IN ONE arm and pulled books from the "your disabled child" section with the other. I was standing in the Coral Gables branch of our Miami-Dade Public Library system. Mikey's stroller was pushed against the stacks, my purse and diaper bag inside. He was about four months old from his due date, or about six-and-a-half months old from the day of his preterm birth. Mark and I spent less time propped on our elbows watching Mikey sleep. During the day, Mikey's eyes tracked our movements. He watched Mark and me, and he would stare intently at his sister and our dog, Cleveland. A few days before, after nursing, Mikey had pulled away from my breast and, for the first time, he smiled a big, toothless grin.

I looked at the books: cerebral palsy, mental retardation, sensory deficits, considering placement for your profoundly affected child. The book titles, tables of contents, and indices rolled over me like a dust cloud. Dewey decimal numbers blurred before me: 616.836, 618.397, 649.152, 618.92. My eyes smarted, and I held my beautiful, injured son close to my chest. I looked into his hazel eyes and saw—or imagined I saw—intelligence and promise there.

What if…what if…I shifted Mikey to my other arm, found a chair, and sat down for a moment. What if I thought a little differently? What if I did all I could to make him a genius or at least gifted? Again, I thought of Dr. Wilker's words back in the NICU: "Numbers are for groups. Your baby is an individual, and who knows how much of a recovery he can make with your help. Genetics help, too."

"There are lots of smart people in our family," I told Mikey. "I'll bet that potential is there for you."

I kissed his head. I knew the usual means of learning might be blocked or hindered by the brain injury. But instead of accepting that he'd be mentally disabled, I thought, what if we strove for mental superiority? Maybe we'd get lucky and break even. And if we couldn't get learning through the usual ways, the eyes and ears, maybe we could get there using other senses, such as smell and taste.

I stood up and clutched Mikey. I went back to the card catalog. It told me the numbers to go to for raising smart children—371.95, 155.45, 649.155. Ah, much better. The dust cloud began rolling away. A cool, light wind of hope opened my lungs. I chose several books and put them in Mikey's stroller. I checked them out, went home, and got started.

I followed many of the suggestions I found in the books and made up a few of my own. For example, I knew the sense of smell is deep in the brain and likely was spared any damage. I took Mikey outside when it was raining gently, so he could smell and feel the sweet drizzle and frangipani-scented air. In the kitchen, holding him close to me, I let him smell cinnamon, crushed rosemary, and fresh mint. His tiny nose wrinkled in disgust when I had him smell an egg I had let go rotten. I couldn't be sure what all this was doing, but I was certain Mikey was receiving information and stimulation.

My friend Mari, whom I had updated on Mikey's progress by phone between her massage school classes, now came over and taught me how to use touch to soothe Mikey's tight muscles.

Mari had been my friend since we were both fifteen years old, when she began dating my cousin, also named Michael. I can close my eyes and see her as she was the first time my cousin Mike brought her into my mother's kitchen: a girl with flaming-red hair, an easy manner, and quick wit. I felt none of the getting-to-know-you strangeness of meeting someone for the first time. She was my sister from the start.

Now, years later, Mari's massage therapist–certified hands worked gently at baby Mikey's back, legs, and arms until they relaxed. His face relaxed too, and he gave her a precious gift: his first laugh. Over the next few weeks, Mari taught me how to soothe and stroke Mikey's tight muscles. I earned smiles and laughs too.

I did more exercises that involved touch, taste, and motion, as well as sight and hearing. I stopped for the day when he turned away or fidgeted, lest I overstimulate him.

Mikey proved his memory was good when he was about eight months past term. I was taking him back to the children's hospital to visit a favorite nurse. Mikey was calm and quiet in the car on the way, but he began to stir as we entered the building. Up the elevator and down the hall to the NICU, he fidgeted. When we entered the unit and could smell the NICU odors and hear the monitors beeping, Mikey thrashed in my arms and began to cry. He wiggled so hard, I feared dropping him. I said a quick hello to the staff, turned around, and ran out. Mikey calmed as the sounds and smells of the NICU faded. I never went back with him.

As the months went on, it became obvious that Mikey had physical disabilities, or, as the medical records said, "sequelae from IVH (intraventricular hemorrhage)." Therapists came to treat him and taught me how to work with the hypertonia (spasticity) in his body. But although his body had difficulties, he seemed to me to be right on target intellectually—even ahead. He was alert and interested. He smiled and laughed appropriately. He looked at Mark when I said, "Where's Papa?"

One morning, when Mikey was about eleven months past the day he should have been born, he surprised us with a gift. We had just finished playing another round of the "Mikey sandwich" game where he lay in the bed between us (the sandwich part) and Mark and I took turns making raspberries on his belly and announcing, "I'm gonna eat this sandwich," as Mikey giggled.

On the bed quilt lay a water-curled paperback of Agatha Christie's *The Labors of Hercules* (I read in the bathtub). Mikey stretched out his right hand to touch it. He patted the cover and said, "Buh."

Mark and I sat up and stared at each other.

"Did he just say 'book'?" I asked.

"What is this, Mikey? Tell me again!" Mark demanded excitedly as he pointed to the collection of detective stories.

"Buh!" said Mikey.

We pointed to a pillow, a stuffed animal, and some laundry that needed folding and asked Mikey, "What's this?" Nothing. Only when we pointed back to the book did he say that precious word: buh. I grabbed Anthony Trollop's *Barchester Towers* off the nightstand and asked again; that, too, was a buh. Generalization!

We unleashed a tsunami of joy at this semantic prowess. Mark and I had him say it again and again. Mikey happily obliged, saying buh with his lopsided smile.

Mark jumped to his feet and scooped Mikey up. Mark began dancing with Mikey while I clapped and chanted, "Book, book! Yay for Mikey! Mikey knows book!"

Mikey laughed at us and bounced about in his Papa's arms. Perhaps he thought his parents were crazy. Our joy was out of proportion to balance our profound sorrow. Everything was writ large with Michael.

CHAPTER 8

Home-Day Party

~~

It had been twelve months since we took Mikey home from the NICU. He was technically one year and two-and-a-half months old, but Mark and I threw a party on Mikey's Home-Day on December 19. We bought an ice cream cake and had friends over for the event. Mikey sat in his high chair, smiling at the attention. Suzi Doucha let twenty-month-old Amy have a little bite of cake. Robin and David Doucha, Amy's older brother, ran laughing through the house. Neighborhood children tossed balloons across the table. Mark and I leaned against each other. The party wasn't fun. We had wanted to honor Mikey's survival, but the party brought NICU memories too close.

It wasn't supposed to be like this. It had been six years since Mark and I were married at my childhood home in Long Island, New York. We had met five months earlier on a blind date arranged by Suzi and Roger Doucha. Roger and Mark were colleagues at WSVN. I was in graduate school at the University of Miami and renting a townhouse from the Douchas in Coconut Grove.

One evening in July 1976, Suzi decided to order pizza for dinner. She was planning to invite me. She looked up Little Caesar's Pizza in her phone diary and noticed the entry for "Londner, Mark," one line below. She had an idea.

"Roger, what about Mark?" she asked her husband.

"What about him?" Roger replied. "I thought you were ordering pizza."

"I am. But Ronnie is short, Jewish, and funny. I think they'd be great together."

Luckily, Roger spoke fluent Suzi, and they got two short, funny Jews together amid the extra cheese and green peppers.

Mark got to the Douchas' house first. When I walked in the room, Mark sprang up from the sofa. He was old-fashioned, standing up when a woman entered the room. I smiled.

Mark and I discovered we both loved Monty Python, Scrabble, and *The Canterbury Tales*. When dinner had turned to crusts, he offered to walk with me across the grass to my townhouse for a game of Scrabble. When I set up the board and we picked our tiles, I saw I had one of my best-ever letter configurations in a startup rack. X O J K B U E. It was my turn first. I had to find a seven-letter word amid those consonants and vowels. I pondered, staring at the rack. Then I saw it.

Got it!" I crowed and looked up at my new friend as I began laying out tiles. I got as far as J-U-K-E when he stood up, knocking over the board as he moved toward me. I smiled.

I reminded him many times over the years that he owed me a game.

The day before we met, Mark had accepted a news reporter job at WKYC in Cleveland, Ohio. He was leaving in two weeks. I thought, "What a shame; I like this guy."

Three days after we met, he asked me to marry him. He got down on one knee in the kitchen. I laughed at him; it was outrageous. About six months later, I amazed myself by marrying this fellow Scrabble zealot and moving into his apartment in a skyscraper in downtown Cleveland. It was fun, blending our little households. We were pleased some of the authors we enjoyed were the same: Kurt Vonnegut, Woody Allen, P. G. Wodehouse. Others were different, as I had lots of Somerset Maugham, Agatha Christie, Guy de Maupassant, and J. D. Salinger. Mark veered more toward historical and political tomes. I had the latest technology, with my IBM Selectric typewriter, and Mark brought a two-volume Oxford English dictionary complete with magnifying glass. I swooned a little when I saw that dictionary set: I knew I had picked the right guy.

After the barely respectable interval of eleven months after our wedding, I had a magnificent baby girl, a puppy named for the city we lived in, and a rented house in the suburbs. A few months later, an offer from Mark's old boss in Miami brought us back to South Florida. With the help of Mark's Air Force veteran benefits, we bought our home. After a few years of doting on Robin, we decided to have another child.

As Mark and I stood together at the Home-Day event we had planned to be a celebration, I watched Mikey with pride at what he was and with sorrow at what he could have been.

"That's our Iron Mike," Mark said.

CHAPTER 9

Let's Have Another Baby—Teddy

THE DOCTORS SAID THE PLACENTAL problems I had with Mikey, who was now about a year-and-a-half old, were not likely to repeat. I wanted another baby. Mark was nervous. I *hakn en a tshaynik* (Yiddish for nagging; literally to break a china teapot). My debate points: all our friends are having babies, Robin shouldn't be alone if Mikey needs lifelong care, and—the clincher—how do you like this negligee? I was pregnant within a month.

As my belly grew, Mikey and Robin were excited about the new baby. Mikey was particularly thrilled. Before the ultrasound confirmed the sex, I was convinced I was carrying a girl. But Mikey always knew it was a boy. He kissed my belly and spoke to "Brother" from the start.

Edward Hale Londner, or Teddy as we called him, was born on Saint Patrick's Day, 1984. He was one month early. As for not having placental problems again, how many ways can a placenta detonate? I had placenta previa (implantation in the lowest part of the uterus, covering all or part of the cervix opening), placenta accreta (pathologically deep attachment into the uterine wall), and a small abruption (tear). Teddy's birth position was all wrong also—transverse (sideways) and breech (upside down). He, like his brother, was born by emergency Caesarean. The last thing I remember before passing out was Dr. Hanft's voice, "It's a boy. Big. Looks good." Then someone else said, "Mother's blood pressure sixty over forty and falling."

I woke up to find Dr. Hanft cheerfully scraping away at my insides. The spinal anesthesia was wearing off, and I stuffed my fist in my hand to keep from screaming against the grinding fire of pain. As the anesthesiologist pumped up the pain relief, I relaxed enough to hear Hanft explain that he was grating my uterus to spare me the hysterectomy usually done in cases of placenta accreta.

A pediatrician friend of Dr. Freund's visited me a day after I gave birth. I was sitting up in the hospital bed, holding Teddy. The doctor looked at the six-and-a-half-pound baby and said he thought his head was abnormal, that the skull plates were fused, and that Teddy's head would never grow normally. He suggested a surgery to put Teflon chips in Teddy's skull to keep the fontanelles open. The doctor then turned and left my hospital room. I hyperventilated with fear and looked at the newborn in my arms.

"I can't go through this again," I thought. "I can't love him." Then I sobbed and laughed as Teddy opened his eyes and looked into my face. "Too late!" I thought as I clutched him to me.

I assailed Dr. Freund with questions when he came to see me. He shook his head and said of his colleague, "What the hell is he talking about? The fontanelle is a little small, true, but we'll just measure his head ear to ear over the crown for a while to make sure his skull is growing okay."

Ted's head turned out to be crammed with excellent, growing brains and flexible fontanelles. He went chip-less.

CHAPTER 10

"Cast a Wide Net": To Sue or Not

A HIGH-POWERED LAWYER OF MARK's acquaintance suggested we consider suing the children's hospital for the ventriculostomy that "exploded" during Mikey's hospital stay. Although the intent of the procedure was to stop the dangerous buildup of cerebrospinal fluid in Mikey's head, the attorney felt the neglect that led the spinal fluid to overflow had harmed Mikey. I remembered how the skull bones in my baby's head had slid over and under each other like tectonic plates during an earthquake. The nurses, usually so warm and friendly, had looked away when I rushed in after receiving the phone call that alerted me to what happened. Shaking, I had asked the lead neonatologist if this accident had caused more brain damage. He had looked away, as the nurses had, shrugged his shoulders, and said, "Maybe not."

So, nearly two years later, when the attorney advised us to consider suing, Mark and I thought about it. The hospital had been negligent. The nurses had been working yet another double shift. The ventriculostomy, a delicate procedure explained reassuringly to us in the days preceding it, had ended with my baby's brain water spreading on the floor like a spilled cup of coffee. I tasted bile whenever I thought of it. I blamed myself for not being in the NICU that night, every night, for the whole eighty days and nights. I kissed that spot on Mikey's head over and over. So, yeah, we were ready to sue.

We met with the attorney in his high-rise office overlooking Biscayne Bay. His cherrywood desk had a Montblanc pen set on it. The Berber carpet on the floor was so thick that we couldn't hear our footsteps as we walked across the room. As Mark and I sat down in the leather chairs, I whispered to him, "Hey, misery money buys a lot." He gave me a tiny, tight smile and reached for my hand. His other hand held a notebook and pen for taking notes.

The lawyer spoke. He nattered on in legalese. "Standards of care…negligence…additional damage hard to prove but expert witnesses…help provide for his care when you two are gone…ease the future burden on Robin…coming up close to statute of time limits for lawsuit…don't delay decision…."

I knew South Florida was a cesspool (or rich resource, depending on your point of view) for lawsuits, especially liability lawsuits like medical malpractice. Mark and I hated to add to this, especially as we knew the vast majority of nurses and doctors at the hospital were caring, competent professionals. Like so many parents, we had bonded with those professionals caring for our child. If we could sue the institution, well, all right. But the attorney said we'd have to "go after" individuals too. The idea of hurting Dr. Wilker made me feel queasy. Even the nurse who should have been monitoring Michael was working yet another sixteen-hour shift and had too many babies to monitor. The institution was at fault for setting this calamity into motion.

Then the attorney made a recommendation that jerked me backward in the plush armchair. Mark dropped the notepad he'd been writing in.

"You've got to sue the obstetrician and pediatrician too. We have to cast a wide net," the lawyer said, leaning forward across his desk to look into our faces.

Mark and I exchanged glances. We had a moment of marital mind melding.

"Like hell," said Mark as he bent down to pick up the notebook, while I said, "No way."

"Now don't get soft and miss this opportunity," the attorney said, frowning and leaning back. "You're not going to hurt them; it's business. There's insurance for this."

"How can we sue Hanft and Freund?" Mark said, also frowning. "They've been wonderful to us. Aside from that, they had nothing to do with the ventriculostomy. They didn't order it and weren't even at the hospital at the time."

I added, "Mikey's middle name is Donald in gratitude to Dr. Hanft. Al Freund has become a friend to our family. My God, we went to dinner with him and Agnes just last week."

The lawyer argued his case to us for a few minutes more. When he saw we were adamant about not suing our friends, he stood up and shook our hands good-bye.

We silently stomped out over the plush carpet, our lawsuit stillborn.

When we told my parents we had changed our minds about the lawsuit, my father was indignant.

"He's not the only attorney in town," Daddy told me. "I certainly understand why you refuse to involve Hanft and Freund, but surely you can find a lawyer who will leave them out."

Mark and I made a couple of phone calls to other law firms, but the answer was the same. We were told various versions of the same line: "You've got to initiate by suing everybody. You might be able to drop Drs. Hanft and Freund later, but you have to at least start that way."

We couldn't stomach the idea of the good people being ground up with the bad—the hurried, careless, negligent people who hurt our child unnecessarily.

I spoke to my father. "Daddy, we just can't sue. The rules of this game are just too miserable. Too many people who did nothing wrong will be hurt. Remember how Dr. Wilker encouraged me while Mikey was still in the NICU?"

Daddy sighed and agreed. "You are doing the right thing; I see that. But you and Mark are lucky you can afford to do it. I'm proud of you both—and ashamed of the legal system."

Mark and I had many a discussion on the facets of doctor, patient, and family communication from our own experience and those of others we spoke with. We shared those feelings with a friend who was on the teaching staff at the University of Miami's medical school. She in turn told colleagues at the school, and eventually we were invited to give two guest lectures in the ethics class. We wanted to title the lectures something along the lines of "Facilitating Understanding between Medical Personnel and Families in Difficult Situations." The ethics professor rejected that—it ended up being called "How Not to Get Sued." The lectures were well attended.

CHAPTER 11

The Birth of the IVH Parents Support Group and PBS: *Frontline* Comes to Visit

In November 1983, *American Baby* magazine published my article "From Anguish to Action" about Mikey's premature birth, time in the NICU, and first two years of life. I received letters from parents and grandparents of other children who had intraventricular hemorrhage, as well as from doctors, nurses, and therapists.

I wrote back to many of the letter writers, and they wrote me again. Many of the questions, concerns, and frustrations expressed were similar. Helen Harrison, author of *The Premature Baby Book*, was one of the first to write me. She was a stalwart activist for premature babies and their families.

After a while, I realized it would make more sense to write one letter in the form of a newsletter and send it out. The newsletter soon became IVH Parents, a small but intense support group that eventually had members on every continent. The concerns of parents in Nashville or Nairobi were often the same. Helen Harrison was vital in her encouragement and support of the group.

All this correspondence turned out to be the swan song for my IBM Selectric typewriter. I'd been lusting for a personal computer since the late 1970s. Finally, Mark and I took ourselves down to RadioShack.

One hour and several thousand dollars later, we had a Tandy 1000A with one 5.25-inch floppy disk drive, 256k of memory (we upgraded from the standard 128k), MS-DOS 2.11, and DeskMate. We also got a dot matrix printer for the desktop publishing of the IVH Parents newsletter. I used the word processing program pfs:Write. There was no hard drive, and we had to switch disks to print or save files. I had a separate phone line installed. We were on our way.

In the spring of 1984, we got a call from a producer associated with the PBS public affairs television program *Frontline*. The series airs in-depth documentaries on a variety of subjects. The producer, Andrew Liebman, contacted us because he was working on a program about how life-and-death choices are made when treating infants with disabilities and poor prognoses. This was during the time of the Baby Doe law controversy.

The Baby Doe federal law passed in 1984. It regulated treatment of seriously ill and/or disabled newborns. The law was controversial because it dictated what must be done for a baby, regardless of the wishes of the parents. The law was a result of several widely publicized cases involving the deaths of disabled newborns who died because medical treatment was withheld. The primary case was a 1982 incident involving "Baby Doe," a Bloomington, Indiana, baby with Down syndrome whose parents declined surgery to fix a problem in the esophagus, leading to the baby's death. The surgeon general at the time, C. Everett Koop, argued the child was denied treatment not because the treatment was risky, but rather because the child had Down syndrome.

Another parent who was being interviewed for the *Frontline* piece suggested Liebman contact us. She knew Mikey's history and that we were vocal in our support of parents' rights to participate in their child's medical treatment.

We agreed to meet with the producer and cameraman at my parents' house in Connecticut. The TV crew videotaped Mark and me at my parents' kitchen table. Mark was serious but informal in his blue polo shirt. I wore a cranberry blouse and an earnest demeanor. The teddy bear necklace I always had on was at my throat.

I told the producer how I thought I was having a miscarriage when Mikey was born so prematurely. Mark talked about how Michael was incapable of supporting his own life, how the machines had to breathe for him. Without medical technology, Mark pointed out, Michael would, indeed, have been a miscarriage. The machines had turned a miscarriage into a life. Then, the narrator spoke.

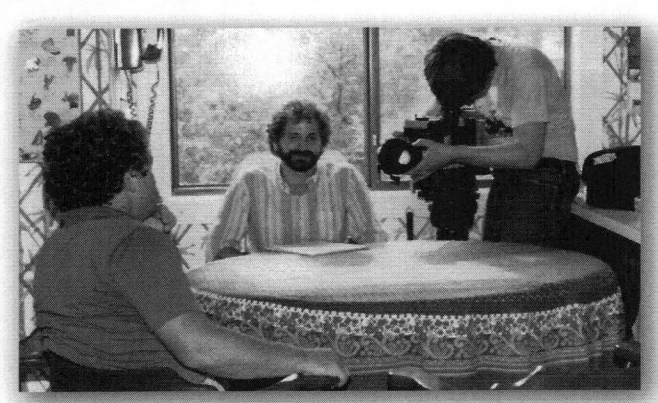

Narrator's voice-over: Michael Londner was born eleven weeks premature. He received the full-court press of modern technology. But Michael suffered a brain bleed, a common complication of prematurity in which a blood leak jeopardizes large areas of the brain. Michael's prospects were grim. But his parents, and even the family pediatrician, found the intensive care doctors unwilling to discuss his treatment.

Ronnie: The prognosis was very bad: severe to moderate retardation; severe to moderate spasticity. I can remember saying to the doctors, "What does the world need another retarded child for? What are you doing?" It was frustrating because we were told that everything was being done to save him and yet what was being saved was probably not going to be anyone who could really enjoy a life.

Mark: It is using the most highly sophisticated equipment to walk into the darkest of forests. And for all the fancy stuff, you haven't got a good flashlight. It was from their ignorance that the physicians were really unable to make any choice except "let's continue doing what we've been doing."

Ronnie: Our pediatrician kept saying all along we should stop treatment, we should pull the plug, we should let this child die, this is too much, it's not right. I'm not saying that that is what should have been done, but we should have had a voice. We should have been able to talk about this more honestly with the doctors.

Mark: At one point, really the critical point in Michael's care, the physicians decided to install a shunt. This is to correct hydrocephalus, which is known commonly as water on the brain. Like all procedures, this one needed a consent form from the parents. We were presented with the consent form. At that point, I said, "While I am not refusing to sign this, tell me what would you do if I refuse to sign it?" The lead physician said, "We'd take you to court and get a court order and then do the surgery."

Ronnie: A lot of this is not looking at the welfare of the child; it is looking after your own rear end as far as the doctors are concerned—they don't want to be sued. They think the parents are making an emotional decision now, they're hysterical, they don't know what they're talking about, therefore we have to make the decisions for them. And they often said, "Well, look, there's plenty of time to die later. We can sustain life and decide later." And there is a point to that too; I can understand that. But then you get to the point where there's no turning back.

Mark: And that's the most unsettling feeling of all, this feeling that you are in a whirlpool and everybody is going down the drain and there's nothing you can do to stop it and you don't even know what's under the drain.

Ronnie: I saved Michael's life myself once. It was instinctive. He was in my arms, in the PCU, in the progressive care unit; he was doing better. He often used to have apnea—he'd stop breathing. I was feeding him his bottle, and suddenly he turned gray and purple and black, and I looked at him and I realized that if I didn't do anything he was going to die right in my arms. And I started, instinctively, to shake him, and I called the nurses and they came over and resuscitated him. And afterward I said to myself, "Did I do the right thing? Is he going to lead such a terrible life that he would've wished that I had let him die in my arms then?"

After the interviews, we went to a nearby playground where the *Frontline* crew taped Mikey and his siblings. It was a lovely, early summer day. Six-year-old Robin played on the slide. Squirrels chased each other up and down the trees. Two sparrows took a bath in a puddle, shaking their heads and tails. I sat on the grass, my face turned to the sun, as three-month-old Teddy snoozed in my arms. Mark and Mikey sat next to us. Mikey was two-and-a-half years old. Mark put out a few toys on the ground, including Mikey's current favorite, a multicolored ball that was soft enough for him to grip. The cameraman just let the camera roll, recording what unfolded in front of him.

After Robin slid down the slide a few times, she walked over to the row of swings. She pushed each of the five empty swings and then ran back to the first swing and pushed each swing again. The rusty hinges squeaked. The producer walked over to her and said, "Robin, we are trying to record here. Please don't make the swings squeak. It will be on the tape."

Robin, ever a TV newsman's daughter, answered, "I know! I thought you'd want some natural sound for the B-roll."

The producer, taken aback, smiled at his miniature "assistant." I heard Mark chuckle proudly. We diverted Robin to the sandbox.

The *Frontline* piece cut to Mikey in Mark's arms at the playground.

Mikey: Papa! Mikey play.

Narrator's voice-over: In fact, Michael astounded everyone. At two-and-a-half years old, Michael's mental development is just a little delayed. He suffers from mild cerebral palsy.

Mark (holding Mikey on top of the slide): On your mark, get set…
Mikey: Go!

Mark held Mikey sliding down the slide as Mikey laughed.

Robin went down the slide. Mikey looked at her and laughed.

Ronnie crept with Mikey on the grass, tossing a ball ahead, both of them creeping toward it.

Mikey: Michael's creeping!

Ronnie: We're both creeping!

Narrator's voice-over: Michael's medical bill came to around one hundred thousand dollars, paid for by the Londners' insurance. But his achievements have been gained mostly because of the countless hours his parents put in helping him overcome his disabilities. Despite Michael's outcome, the Londners still resent being excluded from decision-making. Many children who have grade IV brain bleeds turn out far worse.

Mikey was creeping and whispering to himself, "Get ball, get ball, get ball." He grabbed the ball, looked up, triumphant, and shouted.

Mikey: Hey, hey!

The camera cut to Mark at the kitchen table:

Mark: It's made undiluted joy impossible. There is an element of pain that's always there. You play with your child in the park, and while you're having a good time and he's having a good time, not far away there is a child running after a ball while yours can't. It's made an undertone of pain something that we live with every day and expect to live with from every day here on in.

Ronnie: For every milestone that Mikey meets and every good thing, there is still that pain. As happy as we are that he is finally sitting up or whatever it is, there is that pain of, my God, he was supposed to do this years ago. It never is just pure joy in any of it. We love him all the more desperately for that, but it's a knife twisted in your heart twenty-four hours a day.

The camera cut to Mikey in the park.

Ronnie to Mikey: Can you tell me the colors on the ball?

Mikey correctly identified all of them immediately.

Narrator's voice-over: Recently, Michael's head stopped growing for a period of six months. It was one of the many grim reminders that at any moment his progress could simply grind to a halt. Even so, how can his parents justify that they almost acted to end his life when now he is doing so well?

Ronnie: If we had acted, we never would have known. And we still don't know how he'll be in, say, six months. He could be in very bad shape, and the decision to stop would not have been wrong. Again, it's so hard to give absolute answers; there are no absolutes. I hope people can understand that.

On November 20, 1984, *Frontline* aired the piece, titled "Better Off Dead?" Mark and I were horrified at the name of the piece, but we felt our family and our decisions were presented fairly.

CHAPTER 12

Walk on By

PARENTS ARE DELIGHTED WHEN CHILDREN begin to walk at the usual age. But as one-year-old Teddy made his way cruising along the living room sofa, Mark and I worried about the effect on Mikey. Teddy could now walk holding Mark's or my hand, and we knew the happy day of independent ambulation was nigh. But would Mikey be jealous and resentful that his baby brother could do what he could not? When we would celebrate this milestone in Ted's young life, would we be looking over our shoulders at Mikey's understandable bitterness?

It happened when Mikey was aboard a horse. Now three-and-a half, Mikey had recently started riding at Kiwanis Horses for Handicapped. Therapeutic horseback riding is effective for many disabilities, including cerebral palsy. The movement of the horse between the rider's legs helps develop balance and trunk strength. Other physical benefits include decreased spasticity, increased range of motion, improved respiration, circulation, and sensory integration. But the emotional benefits are also exciting. I loved witnessing the transformation of shy, trepidatious kids clinging to their parents on their first day into eager children, patting their horses and scrambling into the saddle each week.

Usually, Mark or I went to the stables to assist Mikey under the direction of the program administrators. Mikey typically spent about twenty minutes on a horse. He would always pat the horse firmly two times as a thank-you after the last circle around the corral. While Mikey was riding, the other parent was typically at home with Teddy and Robin. But this Saturday, Robin had a playdate, so we decided to go together with both boys. We dropped Robin at her friend's house and headed out to the stables in the Redlands area of Miami.

The sight, sound, and smell of horses have always made me happy. I was one of those little girls who wanted a pony. I still do. I attended an equestrian summer camp for six years, starting at age ten. I'd sing on the bus on the forty-five-minute ride to the camp because I was so glad to be on my way. One of my happiest memories is of lying on a pile of straw in a roomy box stall with Lonesome Road, a gentle bay gelding. The drumbeat of a downpour outside added to the stall's coziness. Lonesome nickered softly, pushing his velvety muzzle into my hand for the oats and carrots I had for him. The rain sharpened the aromas of the sweet straw and hay. I knew the sun would come out soon and I'd tack up Lonesome and ride in the woods, jumping over logs and startling rabbits. It was the bliss of the now and the soon to be.

So, I enjoyed going to the stables for Mikey's horse therapy. He was surprisingly fearless—a tiny boy on a big horse. He had the protection of a helmet and the support of three people: the person who led the horse and two side walkers who held onto Mikey and steadied him in the saddle. As the weeks went by, Mikey needed that saddle support less and less.

Mark led the specially trained horse inside the corral with about six other riders and helpers. I pushed Teddy around in his stroller in the grassy area outside. Teddy fussed as I bumped the stroller over the ground. He turned in his seat, demanded up, and began to climb out. I hoisted Teddy up and put him on the ground, holding tightly to his hand. He'd never been to the stables before, and I knew how he liked to explore.

Teddy and I watched Mikey and Mark make their way around the corral with the other horses, riders, and helpers. Mikey spotted Ted and me and shouted out, "I'm riding!"

Ted yelled back, "Mikey, horse!" He slipped his hand out of mine and began toddling toward the corral, hollering, "Horse, Mikey! Mikey, horse!"

Mikey yelled back, "Brother is walking! Oh yay!" He bounced up and down in the saddle with glee. He turned in the saddle to face his father. "Look, Papa, Brother is walking!"

Mark shouted, "Get him, Ron!" I hurriedly stumbled after Ted, who had suddenly plopped on the grass, looking surprised. I swooped him up.

From my arms, he roared again, "Mikey, horse!" as his big brother yelled back, "Brother can walk!" A few of the other riders and helpers joined in, shouting, "Brother can walk!" We all laughed. Across the dirt, grass, and manure, Mark and I shared a teary smile.

"Not a bitter bone in his beautiful body," Mark told me later as we strapped the boys into their car seats for the ride home. We were amazed and humbled by the generosity of Mikey's heart.

CHAPTER 13

Finding a School for Mikey

FROM AGES TWO TO FOUR, Mikey attended preschool classes exclusively for kids with disabilities. He had some marvelous teachers, but there were gaps in his social and educational life. Mikey was often the only child, or one of the few, with normal speech and intellect. He needed a more well-rounded atmosphere, but he still required support for his physical disability. Mikey could not stand or walk unassisted. His preferred method of getting about on his own was to creep on hands and knees. He got quite good at it, almost a four-point run when motivated. He'd race on hands and knees, laughing his famous belly laugh as he chased a Hot Wheels car. Mark's grandmother, a gifted seamstress, made pants for Mikey with thickly reinforced knees.

Mark and I had been pleased with the nearby Jewish day school Robin had attended at a similar age. I may be more of an ethnic Jew than an observant Jew, but my Judaism is still a central and important part of me. Being a Jew is an extension of family—my extended tribe. I was confident Mikey would be welcomed at the school where his big sister had done so well.

Wrong.

I called the school Robin had attended. We were still members of the affiliated synagogue. I left a message for the preschool director: "Hello, this is Ronnie Londner. My daughter Robin attended your preschool, and we were delighted. My son Michael is now ready for your age-four class. He has cerebral palsy, which is why we have had him at a school for children with disabilities, but he has normal intelligence, and I'm sure he is ready for your curriculum. When can we meet with you to sign him up?"

Director Aleph, as I'll call her, called back. After the pleasantries, she indicated Michael's preschool registration was not assured.

Director Aleph told me, "I'm not going to be here next year, so I'm reluctant to make a decision for another person. Dr. X will be here in July, so it really is his decision. It's hard to predict…it's difficult to tell how it would work out. I tend to think that our physical setup would not facilitate. The classrooms are rather small. There would be about fifteen children, a teacher, and an aide. What is the ratio at Michael's present school?"

"There are seven children, one teacher, and two aides," I replied. "But that's for the zero-to-three class. The ratio at the three-to-five program is much higher, similar to yours. I realize you can't give an opinion for someone else, but I'm curious: If it were your decision, what would you say?"

"My inclination is to try it," said Director Aleph. "Now, that would not be a firm commitment. I'd say let's give it a month and see how it works. I'd have to see the child. It might be a challenge. If there were a combination of mental and physical problems, I'd say no, but since it is primarily physical, I'd say try it. But the teacher must be willing. I have a reservation about the small classroom size. I don't know if he'd have enough room to crawl around. The chairs and tables might get in his way.

"His current classroom is set up like any other," I assured her. "There are tables and chairs, and he simply creeps on his hands and knees around them. He doesn't need great, wide-open spaces."

"If you don't mind," she said, "I'd like to discuss it with our school psychologist and the teacher who'd be in charge."

"That's fine. I'd be interested in what they have to say."

A few days later, Director Aleph called me back.

"Well, I spoke with the appropriate teacher, and she wasn't overly positive, let me put it that way. She's concerned about the classroom structure. She's worried about the reaction of other children and their parents. She's afraid they would resent the extra time given to Michael — time taken from their children."

"Did she actually speak to parents, or is this just what she thinks?" I asked.

"No, she didn't speak to any parents; these are her own feelings. She sees the physical size of the classroom as a problem. It's small, and she worries

Michael and the other children might get in each other's way; the other kids might fall over him."

"They might get in each other's way the first day or so, but they'd soon adjust if given the chance," I said. "I asked Michael's physical therapist and she said she could come to help him and the other children adjust. She could also help Michael learn to use the toilet at your preschool."

"Yes, well, I spoke to the school psychologist also. She recommended two other schools for Michael."

"Did she say anything other than recommend he go elsewhere?" I asked.

"She is concerned about his fine motor skills. Our teachers are not equipped to handle that."

I was quietly furious, but I persisted asking questions. At this point I just wanted to hear what she had to say. "What do you require of three- to four-year-olds? Michael can use crayons and pencils with his right hand. He colors within the lines with a little overlapping. He can draw a circle and an X."

Director Aleph seemed surprised. "He can? I didn't realize. That's terrific. Well, I wouldn't give up. Maybe you should talk to the teacher yourself. And if she could see him, maybe you could convince her."

My anger and disappointment rose, and spilled over into my voice.

"Convince her! I don't plan to send Michael where he is not welcomed with open arms," I replied. "I'm disappointed that a Jewish institution, where my daughter attended, is not interested. I wanted him to have some *Yiddishkeit*."

"I agree," Director Aleph said. "I think it's a shame. I'll talk to the new early childhood director when he comes."

There were a few more calls back and forth, and by this time we didn't want Mikey going there anyway. I did not tell the officials that because I wanted to see how their decision would play out. Two weeks later we got the official word: "We don't feel it would be an appropriate placement." The unofficial word at our house came from Mark: "What schmucks."

We resigned our family membership from the associated synagogue.

I gave myself a few days to cool off. Then I called another Jewish preschool. I'll call its leader Director Bet.

Director Bet's first words were "What kind of palsy does your son have?"

I explained the situation.

"This is very much different from what we have had before. We've never done anything like this. This is a bad time of year for me to think of it. I hadn't given thought to it before. Cerebral palsy, doesn't that mean he shakes a lot?"

"Cerebral palsy does not mean he shakes," I explained. "It means his muscle control was impaired by the brain injury he had when he was born early. He can't walk independently, and his left arm is affected."

A discussion followed on what exactly would have to be done for Michael, such as the need to be pushed in his stroller to and from the playground.

"That's extra work for the teacher," Director Bet said. "I'd have to check to see how their contracts read."

"In some ways it would be similar to a child with a broken leg," I said.

"But this isn't a broken leg; this is forever. Besides, we never had a child here with a broken leg."

I spoke about broadening the horizons of other pupils and teachers.

"It's more than just broadening horizons," she replied. "These children need heartfelt care and attention. There are special education teachers who are trained to work with children like your son. Those teachers have smaller classes, and they make much more money than our teachers."

I corrected her misinformation regarding special education teachers' salaries.

"Well, I've never worked with children like this before. I've never had anything to do with children or adults who were not completely normal. When I see a person in a wheelchair at the mall, I say to myself, 'Thank God that's not me or my children.' How do you adjust to this? I'd need to meet this child. I want to talk to the rabbi about it, and some school administrators. This is completely foreign to me. You must be very different to be able to adjust to this."

"No, I'm not different at all," I responded. "I'm the same person, just like any other person."

A person ready to scream with frustration and disappointment, I thought as I restrained myself from banging the phone on the kitchen counter. What is it with these people, making me out to be different so they can distance themselves?

"But you must be different to be able to cope with this," she persisted.

"No. This kind of thing can happen to anyone at any time," I replied.

There was a slight pause. "Well, I'll get back to you," she finally said.

We were not accepted at that school either. "Cannot meet your son's needs at this time" read this rejection letter. I gave up on Jewish schools and moved on to explore the local Montessori options.

I liked what I knew about the philosophy of Maria Montessori: respecting the dignity of children and making learning fun and often self-directed. She taught that practical chores can be instructive and gratifying, children should have consequences to actions as opposed to punishments, and teachers should respect and respond to different learning styles. If a child needs to walk, pace, or, in Mikey's case, creep on hands and knees while learning, that is generally accepted.

I called Eleanor Winhold, headmistress of the Winhold Montessori School. Mrs. Winhold asked me Michael's age, his abilities, and his interests.

"He sounds like a wonderful child," she said. "Do you want to bring him in and let us look at each other?"

Goosebumps of joy and hope ran down my shoulders. "That sounds great," I said. "Have you had disabled children there before?"

"Not per se, but we do have children with different strengths and weaknesses."

We made an appointment for later that week. I hung up the phone and cried in relief.

When I brought Mikey to our tour at Winhold School, Mrs. Winhold greeted me with a smile and then looked right at Mikey. "Hello, Michael," she said.

Mrs. Winhold showed us the three classrooms that made up this location of her school. Mikey was fascinated by the play kitchen in one of the classrooms. Mrs. Winhold and I talked about how to make her school work for my child. I asked her if she wanted a physical therapist to come to help orient Michael and the other children. She said that might be nice for a few times, but we would see if it would be necessary long term.

"Nice work putting that cupcake in the oven," she called to Mikey, still at the play kitchen. "You're a natural!"

I asked her when I could give her a check for a deposit.

Mrs. Winhold's school gave Mikey more than an education. His new friends invited him to birthday parties and play dates. What a joy it was to see him in earnest conversation with other children or laughing as he dug in the sandbox in the playground. Yes, the other children could run circles around him while he crept from here to there, but if Mikey was laughing so could I.

But despite his sweet smiles and belly laughs, Mikey knew he couldn't do many of the things that would make life easier for him and for others. He made that clear to me one afternoon when the boys and I were running errands school.

We were at the bank. Teddy was about twenty months old, and Mikey was four years old. I was waiting in line to put a check in our account when I realized—as did everyone else in the bank—that Teddy had already made a deposit. He'd thoroughly pooped his pants and the overflow was apparent. I left the line and took the boys into the ladies' room. Ted could walk, and Mikey had recently moved from a stroller to a wheelchair. The restroom door was narrow, so I had to leave the wheelchair outside. I couldn't prop the door, and I wouldn't leave Mikey by himself, so I carried him in one arm and steered Teddy with my other hand.

There was no changing table or similarly convenient surface. So I got on the floor and began to wipe the gluey mess from Ted's legs and bottom. I was also trying to hold Mikey up, or prop him against the wall, so he wouldn't get soiled too. The room was so small you couldn't change your mind in it, much less an exploded diaper. Ted was crying—the floor was cold and he was a mess—and Mikey recognized I was having trouble. He kept sliding down the wall, although he was trying valiantly to stand.

"Mama," he said, reaching out to touch my face, "I hate cerebral palsy." In his four-year-old pronunciation, the words sounded more like "ce-weeb-ill paws-ly."

Mikey knew what cerebral palsy was; he'd heard the term listening in on therapists, doctors, and teachers. He had asked me what it meant, and I told him long ago. I had told him cerebral palsy was why he had difficulty walking and why his left arm didn't work as well as the right.

I clutched him to me now, kissing him over and over and said, "Yah, Mikey, I know. Me too. But I sure love you."

I began to sob, Mikey started crying, and Teddy was already wailing. Someone banged on the door, "Are you all right in there?"

"We're fine!" I answered and giggled at the incongruity of my answer amid the puddles of shit and tears. That set the boys off laughing, and we all survived another day.

CHAPTER 14

It's a Small World

ONE OF THE PERKS OF living in Florida is proximity to Disney World. Mark and I were snobs about many forms of entertainment—we didn't watch much non-news TV or go to rock concerts. But when it came to Disney, we gave over and wallowed in the regimented joy. Like so many parents, we gazed at our children's laughing faces and at each other and couldn't help laughing at the overall delight in the air. When Teddy tried to catch the jumping water in the fountains, or when Mikey leaned forward in his wheelchair, pointing and shouting enthusiastically at a monorail as it sped by ("I want to ride the purple one!"), or when Robin hopped, danced, and pulled at Mark's hand as we neared Cinderella's Castle—we all knew we were, indeed, at the Happiest Place on Earth.

Happiness, like everything else with Michael, meant something different than it did with other children. Going to Disney World with a disabled child meant never waiting in lines. The park arranged quick access for people in wheelchairs. When Robin's friends at school would complain about long lines for "It's a Small World" or "Peter Pan's Flight," she would shrug her shoulders.

Like all families we had our rituals: Orville Redenbacher popcorn before the Haunted Mansion, popsicles under the WEDway People Mover, and cool, tall glasses of stout for Mark and me at the Rose and Crown, Disney's Epcot version of an English pub.

The parks of Disney World were wheelchair friendly, so we had no struggle to find curb cuts and ramps like we did in the real world. We often stayed at the Contemporary Resort, which had elevators large enough for our whole family, including Mikey's wheelchair. Restaurants had tables at perfect wheelchair height. "Cast members," Disney-speak for staff, also made things easy. A little too easy, sometimes. Character performers—the actors inside the Donald Duck, Mickey Mouse, and other costumes—always made a beeline for Mikey. One Pluto in particular, instead of the customary two-minute visit, stayed with the family during nearly an entire character breakfast.

Michael's appreciation for this extra attention depended on his vantage point. If he was in his wheelchair—where even a small character, such as Chip or Dale, would seem towering—he would often cry and reach for Mark to protect him. But if Mikey was on his favorite Disney perch, Mark's shoulders, Mikey would smile and giggle even if a tall character like Goofy ambled over to say hello. Mikey would pat Goofy's muzzle or grab for Goofy's hat.

Robin would circle the character, practically dancing for attention. But, whether it was Disney's training or concern from the individual inside the suit, the walking cartoon character often spent the majority of his or her time with the disabled child. Teddy was usually too busy eating his Mickey Mouse ears–shaped waffle to care or even notice.

Mikey loved trains and could indulge his passion for them at Disney World. At home, he often wore his train engineer's cap when playing in the house. Thomas the Tank Engine seemed to be on constant rotation on the VCR. We bought him a ride-on train set for his birthday one year and laid the track out on the patio. Mikey was the engineer, riding the circuit over and over, while Teddy, the stationmaster, checked his brother in to "stations" announcing, "Tennessee!" or "Alaska, now!"

At Disney World, the monorail that moved guests between hotels and the Magic Kingdom and Epcot was one of Mikey's favorite rides. He enjoyed watching them as well as riding in them. One of the best parts of character breakfast at the Contemporary Resort was the monorail that picked up guests inside the hotel. Mikey would look up from his Mickey Mouse waffle and point at a train pulling into the platform. So excited he couldn't speak fast enough, he'd shout "A—a—a train! A train!" He and Teddy named their favorites. The lime green one was Slowpoke, and the purple was Fastpoke.

Through the Florida resident grapevine, we knew it was possible to ride at the front of the monorail with the conductor. One morning, we pushed Mikey's wheelchair to the front of the platform and waited to speak with the cast member standing there.

"My son loves trains," I explained. "Is there any way we could ride in the front with the conductor?"

The cast member looked at Robin and Teddy jumping in their excitement over going to Epcot as Mark talked to them and held the handles of Mikey's wheelchair. Mikey joined in the conversation. His right hand moved to punctuate his words. His left hand, weakened by cerebral palsy, stayed in his lap.

"Consider it done," the cast member said.

I thanked her over and over and then turned and shouted to Mark, "We can do it! We can ride up front!"

A few minutes later, Teddy and Mikey were sitting on the tan vinyl seat that wrapped around inside the nose of the monorail. The boys' faces were as close to the windshield as possible. The monorail conductor, a serious and competent young woman, welcomed our family and said, "Ready? Here we go!" The boys squealed with delight.

The train started slowly and then quickly picked up speed. Teddy laughed and chattered, but Mikey was seriously and quietly joyous. We were traveling from the Magic Kingdom to Epcot—or as Mark affectionately called it, Schlepp-cot, because of the *schlepping* (Yiddish for carrying something heavy or walking, trudging) Epcot visitors do.

Mark said, "Mike! You like sitting up front?"

Mikey beamed at him and answered, "Yeah!" He braced himself as we zipped through a curve that threw us all back a little.

Mikey turned to his brother and said, "We are going so fast!" They grinned at each other and simultaneously looked out the windshield again as the trees and grass sped by. Teddy leaned over to his brother, embraced him, and whispered something in his ear. I couldn't hear what he said.

Mikey turned to the rest of his family. "It's going really fast!" he said excitedly. Somehow, up front, with the track visibly curving in front of us, the train did seem faster. Mikey, who usually moved by wheelchair or by crawling, so often had to settle for slower speeds than he would like. Now he was zooming along, watching trees and buildings peel off to the sides of the broad windshield.

After a few minutes, the big ball that housed Epcot's Spaceship Earth ride came into view.

The monorail slowed, and Mikey objected.

"I don't want to slow down!" His lower lip came out in the beginnings of a righteous pout. When the monorail stopped, Mark picked Mikey up from the seat and held him close, their heads touching as they continued to stare out the front window. As we stepped onto the platform, Robin excitedly asked her brothers, "Wasn't it great to be up front?"

Teddy answered, "It was so fun!"

Mikey didn't answer. He was busy staring at the train from his father's arms. He had one arm around Mark's neck and the other hand reached out to touch the train. Mark stopped and moved as close as he dared to allow Mikey to touch the gleaming white-and-purple surface.

Mikey stretched his arm as far as he could and patted the train two times, just like he patted the horses he rode on Saturdays. Then my train-loving boy said softly, "Thanks, Fastpoke." He put his other arm around Mark's neck. "Thanks, Papa. I liked it a lot."

CHAPTER 15

Support Groups

My support group, IVH Parents, was useful to me and to others because of its specificity—children who had intraventricular hemorrhages. The group helped connect parents and medical professionals around the world. Even if there were no other IVH children for miles around, these families could still find comfort and information. But that narrow focus was also a weakness: IVH Parents usually couldn't address the local concerns and difficulties of any one child or family.

To help local children with any type of disability, Parent to Parent of Miami was born on my dining room table in 1986. There were three of us there, all mothers: Paula Lalinde's daughter Alex had spina bifida, Linda Machado's daughter Carmen had profound disabilities from a variety of syndromes, and my Michael had cerebral palsy. One of our immediate goals was to help local families get the services, referrals, and support needed to for their children. After all, the cause of a disability is less important than finding out what school a child should attend; which doctors, therapists, and programs could help him or her; and how we parents could help our children have what all kids need—fun and friends.

We three mothers, in creating our new support group, looked to Parent to Parent of Florida and Parent to Parent USA. The first program of its type, Pilot Parents, was started in 1971 by two women in Nebraska, a mother and a social worker. Then, the goal of forming a community where parents of children with disabilities could share information and emotional support was a radical concept. Local Parent to Parent groups, such as the Miami group Paula, Linda, and I spearheaded, were born of necessity as medical science saved the lives of sick and disabled babies but then left us to our own devices on how to raise and provide for our children and our changed families.

We parents and kids got to know each other. We formed a bond of friendship through our mutual struggles.

"It's different from the usual mother-to-mother friendship," I said to Mark one afternoon when I was getting Mikey ready to go to a friend's house. "When we plan playdates, we think about things like seizure medications, wheelchairs, or head support for a five-year-old. It's just easier to deal with when people already understand."

When I agreed to babysit one mother's profoundly disabled child, she cried.

"Everyone else was too afraid," she said. "I love baby April, but my husband and I need a night out."

Being involved with the group helped me find a measure of comfort. In the middle of the night when I would have nightmares about Mikey's brain injury, I knew there were other mothers I could call in the morning who would understand in a way my tremendously supportive husband did not. Talking these things out mother-to-mother helped.

My other group, IVH Parents, continued to evolve. In addition to the monthly newsletter, I answered letters and phone calls from many parents. I'd get calls all hours of the day and night. A mother in Egypt kept forgetting the time difference. Parents sometimes called from neonatal intensive care units in the middle of their nights, not giving a damn what time it was. Doctors, nurses, and therapists called also, thankfully during polite, Eastern time zone business hours.

One of my most asked-for services was to match parents of infants still in, or recently released from, the NICU with parents of older kids with similar medical histories. These new parents wanted a glimpse into their child's possible future, just as I did when Mikey was still in the NICU. Hearing doctors' opinions and morbidity statistics wasn't enough. Although geography usually made in-person meetings difficult and rare, parents could at least speak with families like theirs had suddenly become.

A typical IVH Parents newsletter would include an inquiry like this one:

> Matthew was born at twenty-nine weeks gestation and had a grade 4 bleed his third day of life. He had surgeries for patent ductus arteriosus, inguinal hernias, and V/P shunt placement for developing hydrocephalus. He is on phenobarbital for seizures. He has cerebral palsy which affects all four limbs, but his right arm is nearly normal. Matthew will be released from the NICU soon and is expected to come home within two weeks. My husband and I are terrified. I would like to get in touch with other families whose child has a similar history but is a year or more older. We know there is a huge range of outcomes, but we want to know what might be in store for us.

Sometimes, the child in question was past infancy because the parents had just learned of the group's existence. Although many professional members recommended IVH Parents, including neonatologists and NICU nurses, most parents heard of us from other parents after their babies left the hospital. People also found us through other support groups' newsletters and recent articles and books on prematurity or disability.

A typical inquiry from parents of a child past infancy is this one:

> Clara was born at twenty-eight weeks gestation, had a grade 3 bleed, and V/P shunt, one revision to date. She is three years old, finally can roll over independently, sits unsupported using her arms when propped, and babbles, but she has no real speech. Her cerebral palsy is described as paraparesis, affecting mostly her legs. The latest EEG shows subclinical activity but no more frank seizures. She continues to take anticonvulsants, and we worry the drugs interfere with her ability to learn. She can follow two-part commands, like "pick up the toy and give it to Daddy" if she is supported while sitting. Clara

had early intervention and now attends a preschool program for children with disabilities. She receives physical, occupational, and speech therapies. She is happy and seems to understand. She puts her arms out to us for hugs. What will the future bring? Will Clara be able to live independently? Will she be able to have a life? Her older brother has some behavior problems, and my wife and I are exhausted.

Members of IVH Parents would write in, asking me to publish their responses to difficult questions. But the people who called me on the phone often asked about my own child. People who dealt directly with Mikey—therapists, teachers, doctors—also often wanted a summary of what Mikey could and couldn't do.

I typed a template I could read aloud or give out:

> Thank you for asking about Michael. He is doing very well in the cognitive area. He was tested recently and came out in the kindergarten/first grade level, with some seven-year-old skills. He is four-and-a-half years old! He reads short sentences such as, "The cat is brown." He is fascinated with words and is always asking, "Mama, what does ---- spell?" when he sees new words. He has some subtle visual-motor problems, possibly stemming from the fact that he sees with one eye at a time, and does not have visual convergence, according to the ophthalmologists.
>
> He does not walk independently, but he can use a walker for short distances. He is triplegic, meaning that three of his four limbs are affected by the brain injury. His right arm is his best limb. His main mode of getting around is creeping on hands and knees. He has a borderline chance of independent, useful walking. We are doing all the usual things: physical therapy, horse-riding therapy, and water therapy.

Though I was in contact with parents and health care workers, both locally and internationally, one thing I didn't tell anyone was that I had a secret folder. My "Ideas to Help Mikey" folder was a collection of notions, from the possible to the unlikely. For example, Mikey could walk well by himself in the pool but not on land. What if we used an eyedropper or some other absurdly slow method to drain the pool water over a period of months or even years until he could walk independently without the buoyancy of the water?

Another unconventional idea was to train a large dog to carry Mikey about for the longer distances when he used a wheelchair. Our twenty-five-pound mixed breed, Cleveland, was too small. I got the idea from watching the progress Mikey and other children with cerebral palsy made with therapeutic horseback riding. He'd have the physical stimulation of balance and core muscle training and the fun of riding a dog instead of a wheelchair. I don't know if the plan was practical or even sensible.

Another notion occurred to me while watching my friend Mari massage Mikey. From infancy he flourished under her soothing ministrations. She mixed a few drops of essential lavender oil into the massage emollient. Her voice was soft and low as she began by stroking his shoulders and neck. After Mari worked for a few minutes, Mikey's body would relax, almost unfurl, as the spasticity from the cerebral palsy eased. When the sessions were over, Mikey's movements were more fluid and less restricted for an hour or two. I wondered if there was a way to extend these benefits. I imagined a gently oscillating, electric blanket–type device. It could enclose Mikey's body like a snowsuit or cocoon from the neck down. Infused with lavender massage oil, the device would be able to give Mikey's muscles a gentle kneading, as often as he wanted. He could sleep or rest in it, to give his muscles more time to calm from their spasticity.

These ideas and more sat in my folder, waiting for the day when I could use them to help my son.

CHAPTER 16

Homegrown Research: Why Do Some IVH Babies Do Better Than Others?

Though many IVH survivors had disabilities such as cerebral palsy, vision or hearing loss, or cognitive disabilities, not all the children had disabilities. Many children in our group had no disabilities, and some tested intellectually gifted. Because multiple births are at greater risk for prematurity, some families had two or even three IVH survivors. Sometimes families had children with comparable brain hemorrhages but different outcomes.

I wanted to understand why children with similar medical histories sometimes have such dissimilar outcomes, so I devised a questionnaire for parents to fill out. So much of what happens during a premature or emergency birth is out of parents' control. For my information to have any value, I needed to find a measurable factor that parents did have some control over. I finally settled on breastfeeding.

Nursing can be a struggle for all mothers, but I knew it could be especially daunting to nurse a baby who survived a brain injury. Milk dries up, often despite pumping, while the baby is in the hospital. His or her suck reflex is often weak. The parents or doctors may worry the baby isn't getting enough nutrition through breastfeeding or is using up too much energy sucking. It's easier for the little ones and their anxious parents for the baby to take a bottle. But is it best? Is it worth the struggle to nurse?

I needed to break down the components to try to answer the question. I called Dr. Freund, who was always willing to help me with my myriad of questions.

"What should breastfeeding mean?" I asked him.

"I would think you of all people would know, Ronnie," he answered. "You nursed three babies."

"Four, if you count Amy Doucha," I pointed out, remembering how that halo of red hair helped prime my pump for Mikey's year of nursing. "I'm asking for research purposes for premature babies with an IVH: What is breastfeeding? Is it one month? Six months? A year? Does it mean no formula at all? Does it mean milk from the breast, or can it include milk that was pumped and bottle-fed to a baby?"

"Breastfeeding means feeding at the breast. Why are you trying to make this complicated, Ronnie?" Dr. Freund replied.

I explained my research plans, and Al reminded me that any data would be drawn from a self-selected group of parents, which could certainly skew the results.

"The mothers and fathers who join IVH Parents are more likely to be intelligent and motivated, which can have a global effect on the child, obscuring what we are trying to measure—breastfeeding on development," he said.

"I know," I replied. "I also know women who are able to breastfeed an IVH baby are more likely to be financially able to take significant time away from work. Otherwise, she could be pumping milk and therefore not breastfeeding by my definition. But how do we separate causation from coincidence?"

"We can't," Al said.

We agreed this research would not be up to gold standards. It could, however, be useful to IVH parents and professionals. Al and I designed a questionnaire that incorporated our own definitions.

- Breastfeeding meant exclusive feeding from the breast for at least four months after release from the NICU, factoring in any time needed for relactation.
- The child had to be least two years old past term to be included.

- Children with grade 3 bleeds were looked at separately from children with grade 4 bleeds. I did not include grade 2 bleeds.
- If the child had a shunt or any shunt revisions, that was also factored in because a child could not breastfeed during the surgery and recovery.
- To define disability, I used reports from developmental professionals such as therapists, doctors, and early childhood educators. Formal tests such as the Bayley or Denver were used as addenda to observations by parents and professionals.

Our goal was to discover if breastfed babies in our group had lower rates of intellectual and physical disability than non-breastfed IVH babies in our group.

Filled-out questionnaires poured in with stamps from all over the world. I was reminded every time I unfolded a carefully completed questionnaire that this information came from generous, frazzled parents who had given their scant free time to help me in my research.

When I computed the answers, I found that breastfeeding related to improved outcomes in intellectual abilities but not to improved outcomes in physical abilities. In other words, a mother who nursed a baby with IVH was more likely (but certainly not guaranteed) to have a baby with normal or higher intelligence. But breastfeeding did not seem to influence her baby's chances of having some degree of a physical disability.

I shared my results with the IVH Parents membership. Whatever the feelings of the participants, I had to present what I found. My research was not perfect, but it was more information than IVH parents and professionals had had before, and I hoped it would be useful.

I sent the same questionnaire to every parent who joined after the initial research, and I added new data when applicable. The results remained the same.

CHAPTER 17

Twin Brothers, Separated by Two Years

MIKEY AND TEDDY HAD A close, twin-like brotherhood. When Teddy was old enough to leave his crib for a "big boy bed," we put him and Mikey together in one big bedroom. They had separate beds, but more often than not Teddy would crawl in with Mikey. Many times I found them asleep together in the morning, holding hands.

They bathed together and played endless games in the tub. "Come on, boys, time to get out before you turn into prunes!" Mark would say to them when they balked at leaving the bathtub. The first time Mark said it, Teddy looked alarmed, but Mikey assured him, "It's okay; Papa is doing a joke again. He means our toes are wrinkled from the water." Teddy picked up his foot and fell over backward into the water, trying to examine his toes. Mark and Mikey both grabbed for Teddy, and I helped Mark fish the boys out, wrapping them both in pink towels, laughing and kissing their wet heads repeatedly.

The boys' bedroom was on the other side of the house, so we put a baby monitor in the room. Mark and I had the pleasure of listening in on many lively conversations over a range of topics. They'd talk about things like

Disney World, school, and the news stories their father covered on television every night.

For her ninth birthday, Robin had a slumber party. The boys switched rooms with Robin so she and her friends could have the larger room and the space away from the rest of the family. So some of Robin's friends slept in Mikey's and Teddy's beds, and some of them slept in sleeping bags on the floor. Overnight, the girls got rowdy. They jumped on Mikey's and Teddy's beds and destroyed them.

Instead of buying the boys two, separate beds to replace the damaged ones, Mark and I moved a blue, fold-out sofa into their room. We unfolded its double bed every night. Mikey and Teddy would sleep there together, holding hands. They often fell asleep after finishing their evening conversation; their faces would be turned to each other—inhaling and exhaling, inhaling and exhaling.

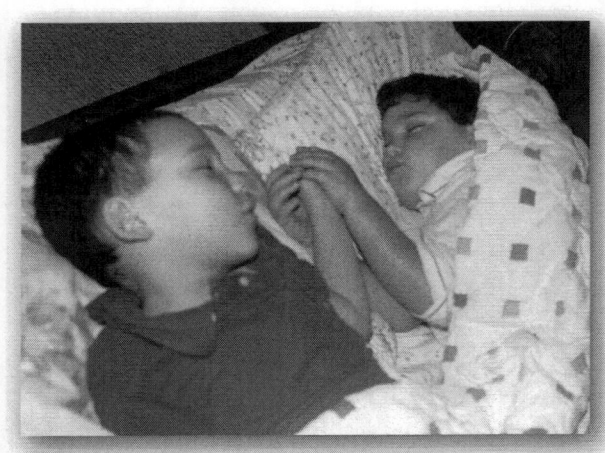

Sweet as they were asleep, Mikey and Teddy awake made a grand team for mischief. Mikey was often the brains of the operation while Teddy, now three, provided the brawn. One of their little schemes went on for who-knows-how-long before it was discovered.

I became aware something fishy was going on when I realized we couldn't keep bread in the house; it disappeared so fast. At first, I thought Mark or Robin was eating it. Maybe they thought I was. And to add to the mystery, I sometimes found a sticky knife in the sink with a few breadcrumbs on it first thing in the morning. I'd put it in the dishwasher and get on making the coffee, mentally blaming Mark or Robin but not giving it much thought otherwise.

Then one Saturday morning I found a piece of desiccated bread behind the toaster. At breakfast, I asked Mark if he knew anything about it. While he vigorously denied any occult toast knowledge, the boys looked at each other and giggled. I thought Mikey looked a little guilty, but Teddy just laughed.

Mark turned to them. "Okay, what do you boys know about this?"

"Nothing!" said Mikey, not meeting our eyes and looking down at his still-full bowl of scrambled eggs.

Robin walked in the kitchen just then to join us and heard Mikey's denial. "You don't know anything, huh, Mikey? Yeah, right." She turned to us with a tattletale's smirk. "They've been having midnight toast parties! I caught them last night."

"What?" asked Mark.

"We have toast parties!" said little Teddy, with equal amounts of trepidation and glee. Mikey glared at him and looked as embarrassed as a five-year-old can.

Michael's physical therapist had warned us the weight he'd gained over the last six months was starting to get in his way. She knew Mikey's favorite foods included bread and pasta and told him—and us—that he needed to cut back on these favorite carbs. She told him things like, "Just one piece of bread in your sandwich, okay, Mikey?" and "When you weigh a little less, it'll be easier for you to do more things."

Mikey agreed, at least in theory. He didn't mind switching to low-fat frozen yogurt or having a bit less pasta. But he missed his bread, especially toast.

"I tell Teddy what to do," Mikey said at his kitchen table confession. "'Cause I can't reach and Brother can."

Now Teddy chimed in. "I got the bread from the freezer! I stand on the schlep stool to reach."

"I'm telling it!" said Mikey, glaring at his henchman. Now warmed up, his declaration of guilt became more like bragging. It didn't help that Mark, Robin, and I were trying not to laugh.

"Okay," said Ted. "You tell."

"So yeah. Teddy gets the bread and takes it and climbs the schlep stool and puts the breads in the toaster," clarified Mikey.

"Oh, my God," said Mark. "The babies are operating electrical appliances alone in the middle of the night."

"You subcontracted to your coconspirator little brother, Mikey!" I said, knowing my smile nullified my attempt at scolding. "You knew you shouldn't be doing this, so you did it in the middle of the night."

Mikey glanced at his father and me, and then he went on. "When the bread is finished in the toaster, then Teddy gots a butter knife and puts jam on, and then we eat it." His tone was triumphant.

"And I throws the knife in the sink!" yelled Teddy, unable to hide his accomplishment any longer.

By this time, Mark, Robin, and I were laughing out loud. I caught Mark's eye mid-laughter, and we shared a poignant telepathic gasp. I knew what he was thinking: the mastermind of this covert, midnight operation had been predicted to be moderately to severely mentally retarded.

"Mikey, how did you figure it all out?" asked Mark, confirming my mind-reading abilities. "You never made toast before. How did you know what to do and how to tell Teddy to do it?"

"Oh, Papa," Mikey said pityingly. "It's easy. I seen you and Mama do it lotsa times, so I just told Brother how."

CHAPTER 18

Barbarism

WE IVH PARENTS SHARED OUR families' stories: our stresses, our divorces, and, when we could find them, our joys.

"Kevin is progressing well. He is two years old now and smiles all the time. We think he is trying to say his sister's name."

"Lola just ran from the kitchen to her bedroom because she forgot her Ernie doll. They said she would never walk! God bless our pediatrician, who always encouraged us despite her big bleed."

"We said we never would try again, but we are pleased to report the birth of Philip James, eight pounds, two ounces. A full-term baby is a joy we never thought we would experience. Baby and big sister Violet are best buddies already."

We also exchanged particulars about the care our children and, by extension, our families, received from medical professionals. Some of that care was very, very good, but some of it was horrid.

A particularly ghastly example was the practice of operating on these tiny babies without anesthesia. This was done without parents' knowledge. Pavulon, the brand name for pancuronium, was used to paralyze babies so they could be cut without being able to move. Pancuronium is a derivative of curare, an arrow poison used by indigenous South Americans to immobilize enemies or prey prior to killing them. The victims cannot move, but they can feel.

Jill Lawson, a mother in Silver Spring, Maryland, discovered in 1985 that her premature son, Jeffrey, had not received any pain relief during an open-chest surgery. Hours after the operation, Jeffrey began a sudden physical deterioration from which he never recovered. He died five weeks later.

When she confronted the physicians, Lawson was told premature babies are too immature to feel pain and too fragile to be anesthetized. When she refused to accept this explanation, she was told to get psychological counseling for her "inappropriate grief response."

Lawson found an ally in John Scanlon, the neonatologist who first cared for Jeffrey after his birth. He was shocked to learn that Jeffrey had surgery without anesthesia. He asked friends and colleagues whether they had heard anything so astonishing. To his amazement, several nurses and doctors said this practice was not uncommon.

"Reasons cited were a belief that newborns don't feel pain and they don't remember the experience," said Scanlon in the 1985 article "Barbarism, published in the *Perinatal Press*.[1] "There is every reason to extend to the newborn the same kind of anesthesia...given to the older child or adult...Stopping pain has an additional benefit because the physiological response to pain can cause a number of physical changes which are acutely detrimental for a sick and unstable newborn. It is way past time to destroy the myth that a newborn has some sort of built-in anesthesia and can't feel pain."

Lawson and Scanlon took the story to the *Washington Post*, which ran an article in August 1986. The headline asked, "Surgery without Anesthesia: Can Preemies Feel Pain?" Parents around the country who discovered their children had also undergone unanesthetized surgery felt they knew the answer.

Doctors began to respond too. Within months of the *Washington Post* article, two major medical journals, the *Lancet*[2] and the *New England Journal of Medicine*,[3] rushed research into publication. The research had been around for some time, and it showed the adverse effects of unrelieved pain in neonates.

---

1 J. W. Scanlon, "Barbarism," *Perinatal Press* 9 (1985): 103–104.
2 K. J. S. Anand, W. G. Sippel, and A. Aynsley-Green, "Randomised Trial of Fentanyl Anaesthesia in Preterm Babies Undergoing Surgery: Effects of the Stress Response," *Lancet* 1 (1987): 243–248.
3 K. J. S. Anand and P. R. Hickey, "Pain and Its Effects in the Human Neonate and Fetus," *New England Journal of Medicine* (1987): 1321–1329.

Helen Harrison alerted me to all this. Her book *The Premature Baby Book* was initially published in 1983 and was the first comprehensive guide to parenting a premature child. She provided financial and emotional support as IVH Parents began and grew. We spoke on the phone fairly regularly. Helen had recently discovered her son Edward had surgeries without anesthesia a decade ago when he was a NICU preemie. She offered to send me the articles she had read.

Helen's manila envelope containing the Lawson and Scanlon articles arrived on a rainy Saturday afternoon. Mark had taken Robin and a friend to Hot Wheels for roller-skating. Mikey and Teddy were napping. The rain was gentle, and the house felt cozy and safe. I slit open the envelope and sat down on the living room sofa. I read the articles straight through.

Even though Helen had warned me, I was dumbfounded. When I finished the last article, I stood up and paced the living room floor. The article pages lay on the coffee table, innocent looking despite their poison. I felt cold now; cozy was gone. I looked at my arms and watched the gooseflesh rise. I burped up something nasty. Was it bile? How could this be? How could someone cut open a baby who felt the knife but couldn't pull away? The thought I kept pushing away burst through: Did this happen to Mikey?

I ran into the boys' room. I knelt at Mikey's bedside and kissed him over and over. He smiled up at me sleepily. I had awakened him for no good reason, and if I kept this up he'd wake his brother, too. Mikey put his arms up, and I lifted him into mine. I carried him down the hall to the master bedroom at the other end of the house. I lay down next to him and held him close. I kissed every surgery scar I could get near. I kissed his stomach. I kissed his chest. I kissed his head in two places.

I dreaded knowing, but I had to find out.

I called Helen after Teddy woke up, and he and Mikey were playing with their train set.

"How did you find out that Edward had surgeries without anesthesia?" I asked her after I rushed through our hellos.

"I got reports of all his surgeries," Helen said. "Not the summaries; you need the complete blow-by-blow of each procedure that includes everything that was done. If administration of anesthesia is not listed there, then it didn't happen."

I thanked Helen for her guidance, while wishing I could return to my ignorance.

"Good luck, and let me know what you find," she told me as we hung up.

When Mark and Robin got home, I showed him the articles and told him of my conversation with Helen. We tried to convince each other this could not have happened to Mikey. We had met many of Mikey's surgeons, and they didn't seem like monsters. We would have known, somehow, if this had happened to our child.

I called Al Freund at home and asked him to get the surgery reports Helen had described. It took more than a week, but he finally got them and forwarded them to me by mail without opening them. This time, it was a sunny Wednesday.

I pulled out the contents of the mailbox and tossed the flyers and bills aside. I grabbed the manila envelope with Freund's return address. I was about to pull the pages out when I hesitated. The kids were still at school. I was alone in the house with Cleveland, the dog. I put the envelope back on the table and sat on the floor next to Clevie. She put her nose in my lap and then rolled over for belly scratches—a familiar maneuver. Usually, I rubbed her belly a few times and then got up, leaving her wanting more. This time I scratched and patted her belly so long that she got up first. She gave me a look that seemed to say, "Enough already. You think I have all day?" I stood up and picked up the telephone.

"Mark, the surgery reports for Mikey got here. I haven't looked at them yet. When will you be home?"

"In about four hours," he said.

"I'll wait."

The time crawled by. I picked up the kids, got them settled, and started dinner. I chopped carrots, celery, and beef and began throwing the pieces into the sauté pan. I stopped cutting. I looked at the cow's flesh I was slicing and put the knife down. I picked the meat out of the pan and gave it to a surprised, and no doubt grateful, Cleveland. I got tofu from the refrigerator.

When the little Honda pulled into the driveway, I was out there waiting for Mark with Mikey in my arms and Teddy standing next to me. We went in the house together and Mark embraced Robin, who was working on her multiplication homework on the dining room table. The boys went back to their Disney video in their bedroom. Mark and I went to the kitchen where the open manila envelope still lay on the table, sealed. Dinner bubbled on the stove.

Mark took the lid off the saucepan and inhaled.

"Vegetarian tonight? Mmmm, smells good," he said.

"Thanks," I replied. "I hope it will taste good by the time we eat it."

I poured us each a glass of wine. We sat down at the table, and Mark pulled the pages out of the envelope. He read them and passed them to me. I read quickly, then slowly, then not at all. I put the papers back in the envelope. Silently, we stood up, walked to each other, and embraced. I felt his shoulders shake as his sobs began. Somehow, his tears delayed mine, as though he was crying for both of us. His sorrow allowed my anger. It was as though we were one person having two distinct emotions.

"Oh, Mikey," he moaned. "It's Auschwitz again. Medical experiments."

Mark's grandmother was in her early forties when she was sent to Auschwitz. Josef Mengele, the infamous Nazi doctor, was one of the physicians who supervised arriving transports of prisoners, determining who was to be gassed immediately and who was to become a slave laborer. He took turns with other SS physicians at Auschwitz in meeting incoming prisoners at the camp. He was on duty when Grandma arrived. When she got to the head of the line, he looked her over and asked her age.

"Thirty-two," she told him, lying by about ten years. Grandma knew her usefulness as a worker would be her only hope. Mengele pointed to the line for slave labor, not to the line for immediate death.

Grandma had survived the war, but, in lying to Mengele, many people believed she had been smart enough to lie to the devil. Mengele was notorious for performing human experiments on camp inmates, including children. I knew Mark was thinking of this as he wept. Grandma, during her time in Auschwitz, had outsmarted her devil more than once, but we hadn't outsmarted ours.

"Mark," I said, "this wasn't medical experimentation. This wasn't purposeful cruelty. This was arrogant, ignorant doctors who preferred to think pain wasn't real. How were you and I even supposed to know this could happen?"

Then it was my turn to cry, and Mark held me.

Hearing the unusual noises from the kitchen, Robin and Ted ran in and Mikey crept in as quickly as he could. All three of them looked at Mark and me. Their eyebrows were bunched, and their mouths were frowns of concern.

"Why are you guys crying?" Robin asked.

"We were thinking about when Mikey was in the hospital, when he was first born," I said. "It made us sad that he couldn't come home right away."

Mark moved to hug Mikey, and his arms embraced Robin and Teddy too. I followed and tightly held onto my family. I gulped back the sobs my body was trying to force out.

Suddenly, I smelled something burning. I turned my head to the stove. The tofu stew was smoking.

"How about pizza tonight?" I asked the kids, as I scraped the crusty mess into the trash.

"Yay!" shouted three happy voices.

A few days later, Al Freund and I talked. He, like most doctors who didn't work in a neonatal intensive care unit, had been unaware of this practice. He was horrified. He expressed his feelings clearly, an endearing character trait: "Preemies don't feel pain? What crap. If they believe that, why are some surgeries done with anesthesia and others not?"

This question loomed large. Helen gave me Jill Lawson's phone number, and Jill and I were soon in touch by phone and mail. The parent-doctor team of Jill Lawson and John Scanlon initially had the same question Al Freund, Mark, and I had—but now they had an answer.

"John and I learned that it is more difficult to administer anesthesia to premature babies," Jill told me. "It takes special training and monitoring by the anesthesiologist. It's easier to do the operation without, especially if you delude yourself into thinking the baby doesn't suffer. Often, even the surgeon doesn't know the baby hasn't had pain relief. Pavulon ensures the baby won't move. The baby can't tell anyone, and most parents never think to ask."

I thought back to the pre-op talks with doctors before Mikey's many surgeries. The talks were about what would be done, why it needed to be done, recovery times, and possible outcomes. I would have thought to ask if anesthesia would be given as much as it would have occurred to me to question if the surgeon would be sober or wearing gloves. Anesthesia seemed a given.

When I found out Mikey had been subjected to this barbarism, I went back to the children's hospital to ask the head of neonatology how this could happen. I did not make an appointment.

He remembered me. I found him in the unit, talking with one of the NICU nurses. "Excuse me, Dr. X," I asked. "I'd like to ask you a question." I stood facing him. The nurse he had been talking to was behind him, out of his line of vision, but face-to-face with me.

I showed him the surgery reports that indicated Michael had had three surgeries with anesthesia and two without.

"Why, Doctor? How can this be?"

He looked at the paperwork and then raised his eyes to me.

"You see, Mrs. Londner, babies of this gestational age don't feel it. The nerve endings are immature and incomplete."

I heard a low sound, a cross between a "humpf" and an "oy." It was the nurse, staring at me from behind the doctor and slowly shaking her head. I thought I saw her mouth the word "bullshit."

I let a tiny, tight smile cross my face to thank the nurse. I didn't dare do more—I didn't want to expose her frankness to Dr. X.

"But, Doctor," I went on, "we've all seen the tiniest babies cry and pull away from heel sticks. They obviously feel pain."

"No," said the doctor. I heard a squeak. I looked down. The doctor's sneakers were in motion. His heels swung back and forth, but his toes stayed on the shiny linoleum floor. I briefly thought he was trying to escape. "That's just a reaction to the stimuli, not genuine pain," the doctor continued, his voice calmer than his feet.

I felt my stomach ball up. Everything felt shadowy and unreal. Silently, perhaps rudely, I stepped around the doctor to leave the unit. I passed the nurse on my way out, and we briefly touched hands. My enraged tears nearly escaped, but I forced them back. Instead, I walked as quickly as I could down the long hall, into the elevator, down more halls, and at last out of the building into the parking lot. I waited until I was in my car to put my head on the steering wheel and cry.

Over the next months and years, I joined with many others who fought to expose this disgrace. We wrote articles, had conferences, and disseminated information.

I heard of parents who tried to get dog tags for their babies so they could ask the American Society for the Prevention of Cruelty to Animals to protect their child as animals are protected from vivisection.

As John Scanlon said in the Barbarism article, "Veterinarians anesthetize small animals for surgical procedures. The human newborn should at least be afforded a similar consideration."

Jill Lawson stated in her article *Standards of Practice and the Pain of Premature Infants from Zero to Three*, "The doctor who failed to mitigate the pain of our son also caused our whole family pain. We have to remember Jeffrey with a world of hurt. Our son is dead, and we can live with that. What is so hard to live with is his life."

Changes were made over time in different medical centers and by different physicians, but it would be many years before the issue was fully addressed.[4]

---

[4] Dr. Jeana Havidich and Dr. Ted Rosenkrantz, "Perioperative Pain Management in Newborns," Medscape (July 22, 2013): http://emedicine.medscape.com/article/980222-overview.

CHAPTER 19

Freckle Feet

PARENTS ARE INTIMATE WITH THEIR children's bodies through the loving care we provide. The smell of our own clean babies is ambrosia. We know the nooks, crannies, and folds of their limbs, the hurricane swirls of hair on the crowns of their heads; we know their starfish baby hands and their velvety cheeks. But sometimes, we can still be surprised.

The five of us Londners spent many a happy hour in the family bed. Weekend mornings, Mark and I often awoke at sunrise to the chatter, chirp, and squawk of the marvelous bird life outside our South Florida home. We dozed, mumbling about whose turn it was to make the coffee and get the newspapers, until we heard the kids trooping down the hall to us. Robin and Teddy would run in, their bare feet slapping against the tiled floor. Behind them, we would hear the slow, determined, four-point shuffle of Mikey's hands and knees creeping down the hallway.

Rob and Ted would bound into our room and bounce onto the bed. When Mikey finally arrived, he would fling himself against the side of the bed and put his arms out for Mark to haul him up and plop him between us. Robin and Teddy oscillated between the foot of the bed, off the bed, back on the bed, jumping down, and in and out of the bathroom. Mikey would lie quietly, snuggled between us. He was not to be dislodged from his place of favor.

One Sunday morning when all the children were on the bed at the same time, Mark noticed that Robin had a freckle on the bottom of her left foot. He showed it to Robin, and he laughed, saying, "How come we never noticed this before, Freckle Foot?"

Robin smiled and clutched her instep, proud of her distinction.

Teddy piped up, "I wanna be a Freckle Foot too!" He thrust his right foot in my face.

I looked. Nothing. But then I peered at his left foot and, lo and behold, a freckle!

"Teddy Bear," I announced, "You are an official Freckle Foot too!"

Ted smirked. "I knew it!"

Mikey, lying between us, regally raised his leg. "Check me!"

Mark peered at the bottom of Mikey's left foot.

"I don't believe it!" he exclaimed. "You too, Mikey! You are all left-foot Londner Freckle Feet!"

Sure this was a Darwinian trait of familial superiority, Mark and I checked each other. Alas, freckle-less.

Were they all born with freckle feet, and we somehow never noticed? Or did the feature emerge recently and perhaps simultaneously?

Some families turn out children stamped with one face. Ours didn't. Robin has her father's features: large eyes and a small mouth. Mikey had my high cheekbones and full lips. Teddy has my eyes and Mark's mouth. The three Londner children definitely didn't look the same…except for the bottoms of their feet.

CHAPTER 20

Drones Club

LIONS GROUP IN PRIDES, HORSES run in herds, and cheetahs gather in coalitions. People group in nations, ethnicities, tribes, and families. Within families there can be subgroups, dynamic configurations that change with circumstances or time. A typical subgroup could be the parents, or it could be the children. It could be the males or the females. It could be those who love Star Trek and those misguided souls who prefer Star Wars.

In our family, we're all Star Trek fans, but other groups emerged, grew, and shrank. Mikey and Teddy enjoyed each other as peers, but as the older brother, Mikey often took on a mentoring role.

One day when Teddy was a few months shy of three years old and Mikey was five, they were sitting in Robin's room while she was away at a friend's birthday party. Like many lively children, they liked to be where they weren't supposed to go. Robin was protective of her Cabbage Patch dolls—that is, her Cabbage Patch Kids—so naturally the boys were curious. The dolls were lined up on a shelf in Robin's closet, out of the boys' reach. They were discussing the relative merits of the collection.

I was in the bedroom across the hall, and I could hear their conversation.

"See dat one?" said Mikey. "It's the ugliest."

Teddy replied, "I like dat one. It's horrible."

They laughed and pushed each other playfully. I was peeking in the door by this time.

"I think the ones on the right side are more horrible," said Mikey. "The ones on the left are a little bit cute."

Teddy crunched up his face and asked, "How do you know which is the right side and which is the left side?"

It wasn't unusual for Ted to ask his older brother for instruction. Mikey had taught Teddy his letters and numbers when Ted was about two. Mikey delighted in teaching. Ted solemnly absorbed it all, asking the occasional question when he needed clarification. Now he wanted his big brother to teach him right from left.

Mikey picked up Teddy's right hand and instructed: "See, this hand is closer to Robin's closet. That's your right hand." Mikey scooched around the floor on his bottom to Ted's other side and picked up his brother's left hand. "And this hand is closer to Robin's bookcase. That's your left hand."

"Oh!" said Teddy, smiling. "Yay, now I know."

I smiled to myself, trying to lurk in the hallway where the boys wouldn't see me. I didn't want to interfere with this instructional workshop. "How clever," I thought. Then Teddy frowned and asked an even more clever question.

"But what if I wanna know which is right and which is left, and I'm not in Robin's room?"

"Ooh, tough one," I thought. "There goes that."

But Mikey didn't miss a beat. He answered, "Just close your eyes, and see Robin's closet in your mind. Then you'll know."

Teddy's frown melted, and he nodded at this explanation.

Neither boy ever had a problem telling right from left.

Another family subset was the all-male configuration of Mark, Mikey, and Teddy. This group acknowledged their subtribe, and Mark even named it. He dubbed it the Drones Club, after P. G. Wodehouse's fictional gentlemen's club in Edwardian London.

Many a Saturday or Sunday morning, Mark would call a meeting of the Drones Club to order. The agenda usually included a trip to Wagons West, a beloved greasy spoon. Robin and I usually stayed at home, breakfasting demurely on Cheerios, reading the *Miami Herald* stories of the day, Dave Barry's column, and the funnies.

By the time I would move on to the *New York Times* Op-Ed page, the boys would come parading back in the house. Ted usually ran on ahead. Mark would follow, carrying Mikey, who would be giggling as Mark sang the latest Drones Club anthem—anything from "Hip to Be Square" and "Take Me Out to the Ballgame" to "Rule Britannia."

Preceding, surrounding, and clinging to the boys was the unmistakable reek of the chili-cheese-and-onion omelet one or more of them had recently consumed. It often took a dose of white vinegar in the laundry water to get their clothes smelling fresh again.

Mark and Mikey made their own subgroup. Their closeness and love were palpable. The children called me "mama" and their father "papa." Mikey frequently called Teddy "brother." But for some reason, Mikey often called his father "friend." He was the only one in the family to do that.

If the children were in their rooms or sitting on the floor playing when Mark came home from work in the evenings, Teddy and Robin typically jumped up and ran to meet him, yelling, "Papa's home!"

Mikey would drop to his hands and knees and creep so fast it was all-fours running. When he got close to Mark, he would stop, get up high on his knees, fling his arms out, and shout, "Friend!" His right arm stretched all the way out, the left only partly, due to the spasticity that was more pronounced in that arm.

Mark would bend down and scoop him up. At seven years old, Mikey weighed about sixty-five pounds, and scooping was accompanied by grunting. Once in his father's arms, Mikey would put his face next to Mark's, and the two stayed cheek to cheek for a sweet moment. Mark's mothering back in the NICU had forged this intense bond.

CHAPTER 21

Mark's Words: On Fatherhood

ONE OF THE ARTICLES MARK wrote for the IVH Parents newsletter articulated how his intense relationship with Mikey changed his view of fatherhood.

> We were at the park. All around us strong, carefree little boys were running and jumping with their fathers, playing catch, tossing footballs, kicking soccer balls.
>
> And it hurt. It hurt because I knew my boy and I would never do these things together. I assumed that because my boy was handicapped, our father-son relationship would be different, abnormal.
>
> I was right. My son and I would never play soccer together. He would never be able to run to catch my forward pass. Our relationship was abnormal. Abnormally affectionate and loving, it was different from the stereotypical arm's-length father-son relationship.
>
> Because of my disabled son, I never thought of fatherhood the same way again. When a child is diagnosed with a disabling condition,

the entire family changes. Feelings of grief, fear, and other forms of stress put tremendous pressures on Mom, siblings, and Dad.

Problem is, fathers—traditionally—aren't supposed to show how much they hurt. Dads aren't supposed to cry. They're not supposed to share confidences. They are supposed to suck up their guts and get the job done.

When confronted with the reality of a chronically sick or disabled child, many dads try to follow that outdated, stiff upper lip prescription. They keep their emotions bottled up—and wind up hitting the bottle, hitting their wives, or hitting the road. Practically any parent support group meeting will yield stories of men who deserted their families or became self-destructive because they couldn't deal with the new challenge to their "strength."

Men who are strong enough to admit their fears and voice their frustrations stand a better chance of actually getting the job done. The "job"—being a loving parent.

Fathers now are expected to be more affectionate than they used to be. Dad isn't there just to administer discipline anymore; he's there for kisses too. You've come a long way, Dad, but society still imposes limits on fathers' involvement, especially when it comes to disabled children.

Often, necessary services—medical, therapeutic, educational—are available only when Dad is at work. That's a source of frustration for two reasons: 1. It restricts Dad's ability to learn about his child's problems and progress. And 2. It creates guilt and uncertainty—Dad is torn between going to work or being present for an important medical appointment.

The way we live and work these days puts tremendous pressure on parents in general, but especially on parents of children with special needs. There's never enough time for housework and outside work; and typically, of course, it's still the woman who handles the housework even though both parents have jobs outside the home.

While both parents are under pressure, the father often feels he's under special pressure: money pressure. Men don't have to protect the family from wild animals any more, but they're still expected to protect the family from financial woes.

It's spelled $-t-r-e-$-$, and it can be a crushing burden for the father of a special needs child. A disabling condition is always expensive. Doctors, therapists, medications, special equipment—there seems no end to the bills. And no end to the insurance hassles. And no end to the worries: What if I get laid off? What if the insurance company stops paying for a particular therapy? Will my boss try to get rid of me because his employee insurance premiums are too high? If I try to change jobs, will I be able to get new insurance? Can we ever start saving money for the future?

Many men find it hard to voice their fears about someday being losers as breadwinners. They're scared to be regarded as wimpy. Talking about it is even worse.

And there's a crucial difference between a woman's stress and a man's stress. It's considered all right for her to share her problems with others, but men feel they have to keep their problems inside.

Only by breaking out of their isolation—only by sharing their anxieties—can fathers hope to stay on an even keel. Some men are lucky enough to be able to share their feelings with their wives. Some have unusually close and understanding friends. But many others need the atmosphere of common concern provided by a support group. Many fathers will open up when they are sure they're around other men who've "been there," men who can identify with the unique problems and pressures of fathering a child with special needs.

There is a place for stereotypical male behavior when it comes to raising a sick or disabled child. Just as women often can teach men how to be tender, men can often teach women assertiveness. Assertiveness—a trait we often associate with men—is vital when dealing with people who provide services to children with special needs.

Like people in any other walk of life, health care and social service providers sometimes can be indifferent, insensitive, or lazy. It may take a bit of old-fashioned male aggressiveness to get questions answered or action taken. Sometimes the mere presence of a father will make doctors or other professionals more attentive.

It's often the case that women—because they were taught as girls not to appear aggressive—are too timid to ask questions and too afraid to insist on answers. My wife, who is active in support groups for special needs children, says that when it comes to dealing with professionals who patronize women, her advice is, "If you can't bring a man, *be* a man!"

CHAPTER 22

Skin So Soft

NEARLY ALL BABIES AND CHILDREN have exquisite skin, but Mikey's was exceptional. The Sephardic blood on my side of the family comes out in some of us as smooth skin and soft hair. My mother certainly has it. Mikey inherited her delicious skin and hazel eyes.

His soft feet hadn't been toughened by walking. Only the skin on his knees was rough from creeping on the tiles and carpets at home and at school.

I was still carrying him on my hip when he was in second grade, far longer than able-bodied children get to ride. When Mikey graduated from Winhold Montessori after kindergarten, we moved him to the Children's House Elementary School, another Montessori program. He brought home spelling tests with "100 percent" written on them, and he learned multiplication and division. Because his fine motor skills were affected by cerebral palsy, his handwriting was poor. His teachers encouraged him to use a typewriter at school, and he used a computer at home. At lunchtime, Mikey would sit with his friends, chatting and laughing together.

In the parking lot before and after school, I often ran with him on my hip because it made him laugh. I could have dragged his wheelchair out of the trunk and used it, but when I carried him, Mikey would hold tight around my neck, bouncing and giggling. I kept one arm around his waist, and the other held his soft freckle foot. My low back would sometimes ache afterward, but I ignored the pain.

We did use Mikey's wheelchair for longer distances, though, and he found unique ways to make the wheelchair useful. When his second-grade class put on a performance about explorers, he played Queen Isabella giving Columbus money for his ships. He memorized his lines quickly, and Mikey's wheelchair made a fine throne for Columbus to kneel in front of. He loved it and would perform at home. By this time, both my parents and Mark's mother and her husband had moved to Florida, and Mikey would give his shows at their houses too, using my mother's lace tablecloth as a mantilla. Teddy would stand in for Columbus at these on-the-road shows.

The performance bug extended to jokes. Telling them or hearing them, Mikey's laugh went beyond belly to whole body. A favorite was the one about the penguin and the baseball game:

> A policeman saw a man walking down the street with a penguin. He told the man he should take the penguin to the zoo.
> "Good idea," the man replied, and off he went.
> The next day the policeman saw the man again, and he still had the penguin with him.
> "I thought I told you to take that penguin to the zoo."
> "I did," the man replied. "We had a great time. Today I'm taking him to a baseball game."

When Mark first told that joke to Mikey, they both enjoyed it enormously. Mikey insisted on hearing it again and again. One day Mark said, "Mikey, you've heard that so many times—you tell me for a change." And so he did—over and over. Each time Mikey would laugh like it was new. And so did Mark.

"One of the pleasures of parenthood is that the old becomes new again," I said to Mark.

Mikey liked to sing too. He sang nursery rhymes, '80s music ("Hip to Be Square" was a favorite), and songs from *Sesame Street*. One day, he roamed around the house singing "Happy Birthday" to various people and things. He sang to me, to Teddy, to Cleveland the dog, to his stuffed animals and toys. He came into the kitchen where I was making bread and sang "Happy Birthday" to his hands. I asked him how old his hands were. He said the right one was six years old (like him) and the left one (the one affected by cerebral palsy) was only two. I rinsed my floury hands, and I held Mikey, kissing each hand many multiples of its age.

Like all of us in the family, Mikey was a great talker. He was curious about words and asked what unfamiliar ones meant. When it came to conversations, Mikey didn't limit himself to English. He was learning Spanish at school, and he took to it enthusiastically. It was almost as though the *nueva lengua* was inside him all along.

I witnessed a particularly heartwarming example at a school event. The children had written and performed an opera and now were having postperformance refreshments with their audience of parents and grandparents.

Mikey was among several children sitting at a picnic table under the spreading banyan trees on the school campus. A classmate's grandmother sat between him and her granddaughter on the other side of the bench. Like many first-generation Cuban Americans, the older woman spoke very little English. Mikey, who had not met her before, said, "Hello."

She answered, *"Hola."* Mikey's face lit up, and he leaned closer to his schoolmate's *abuela*.

"¿Te gustó la obra?" Mikey asked.

"Sí, fue excelente," answered the *abuela*, smiling at him and moving closer. As they chatted on, I noticed that Mikey, who was often shy with strangers,

was utterly comfortable. He touched the lady's hand. She reached over, patted his hair, said something I didn't catch, and they laughed together.

In this moment I got a glimpse of a different, future Michael. His manner was courtly and grown-up. He was at ease, speaking another language with someone he had just met. He was his own man, separate from me, moving through life with confidence and grace.

CHAPTER 23

Mikey's Secret

Seven-year-old Mikey had been keeping a secret. For months, he and his physical therapist had been practicing something behind closed doors. When I would ask Orlynne, the physical therapist, why I heard so many giggles during their twice-weekly sessions, she and Mikey would smile at each other.

"It's a secret, right, Sissy?" Mikey said, using his special nickname for Orlynne.

One December day, all of us parents and grandparents were gathered on the patio. Orlynne had told us to be ready for something special. Jimmy, her husband, came along to take video. We chatted, speculating about the big surprise.

"Here we go," Orlynne's voice boomed from one side of the patio.

Then, for the first time, we all saw Mikey walk with crutches. Focused, fearless, he placed his crutch and stepped toward Mark. Then he placed the other crutch and took a second step. Slowly, but methodically and confidently, Mikey placed and stepped and stepped again, and then again until he walked the fifteen feet from his starting point to Mark's arms.

Mark cried. He later told me his tears were of pride and sorrow.

"It was sorrow that something so easy for other children was so difficult for my child," he explained. "It was pride that my son would work so hard to achieve a goal."

Mark folded Mikey into his arms. The grandparents and I cheered. Robin and Teddy clapped. Orlynne grinned, and Jimmy kept recording. But Mark kept crying, holding Mikey chest to chest. Finally, Mikey pulled away.

"That was our secret," he told his father, motioning to Orlynne. "We have been practicing and practicing."

Mikey crutched his way over to his grandparents and me. We gave hugs and kisses and tried to hold back our own tears. But Mark, who began mothering Mikey in the NICU, cried until Mikey crutched back over to him.

"I did it, Papa," Mikey said. "I did it!"

"Yeah, Mikey," Mark said, finally able to stop his tears. "You are tremendous."

CHAPTER 24

Mikey Tells Teddy Something Important

⁓

I COULD HEAR MIKEY, EIGHT years old, and Teddy, a few months shy of six, talking in their bedroom across the house. The baby monitor we installed for safety allowed us to listen as the boys discussed various subjects before they drifted off to sleep.

This night, in early January 1990, the boys were talking about the Sandinistas in Nicaragua. Mark had been covering the story for WSVN, and the topic had been dinnertime conversation. Mark was out of town that night on an assignment, and I made a mental note to tell him about the boys' endearing, grown-up talk when he came home. I was drifting off to sleep when suddenly Mikey changed the subject.

He said to Teddy, "You know, I have to die soon."

I sat up in bed, startled.

Teddy said, "No, I don't want you to."

I grabbed a nearby notepad and pencil and began transcribing what the boys were saying.

Mikey said, "I know, but I have to. I have to, Brother, but it's okay."

He did not sound cheerful, but he certainly did not sound distressed. It was as though he was talking about having to go visit a less-than-favorite relative.

"No!" replied Ted, and I could hear the stubborn pout he had in his voice when faced with something he didn't want to do.

Then they began talking about something else. My heart was pounding. I ran into their bedroom to check on them, and when I got there they were both drifting off to sleep. I looked at Mikey, put my hand on his chest, and felt his strong heartbeat. He seemed fine. He smiled at me sleepily. I kissed his cool forehead. Finally, I went back to my bed, looking over my shoulder at my thoughts down the long hallway. Should I go back? Should I wake Mikey and ask him what he meant? Should I call Mark?

I didn't do any of those things. I pondered the incident for a day or two, and I told Mark about it when he got home.

"Children can say strange things," he said, his voice not as confident as his words. "Remember when Mikey was two years old and he talked about helping your father in World War Two? Remember when Robin was three and she said she was your mother's mother?"

"Yes," I replied. "But Mikey is eight, not two or three."

Mark paused. "Yes," he finally said. "But Mikey seems fine."

After a week or so, I stopped thinking about it. Six weeks from when he told his brother he would, Mikey died.

CHAPTER 25

Ear Infection

⁃⁃

DR. FREUND DIAGNOSED AN EAR infection when I brought Mikey in when he complained of a headache in mid-February 1990. Al prescribed the pink, gooey liquid amoxicillin that Mikey didn't mind taking.

Michael was no better the next day. I called, and Dr. Freund said, "Continue the medication, and bring Mikey in again if he's not better by tomorrow."

Michael slept nearly the whole day away and didn't want anything I offered him to eat. That evening, after Mark got home, Robin and I ran out to TCBY to get Mikey his favorite frozen yogurt—chocolate and vanilla swirled in a cup. I went into the boys' bedroom with the treat, anticipating Mikey's happy smile when he saw what I had for him. But he lay in bed and didn't answer when I called to him and gently shook his shoulder. I went into the kitchen and put the frozen yogurt, plastic spoon and all, into the freezer and went back to look at Mikey again. I brushed his soft hair from his forehead. He didn't move. His sleep was too deep, too still. Just as I was looking for the phone to call Dr. Freund again, Mikey suddenly stiffened. His head and neck arched back as his body planked.

A cold sweat dripped down my back. I'd never seen this, but I knew it was bad.

I shouted to Mark, and he sprinted into the room, propelled by the shrill timbre in my voice neither of us had ever heard before.

Mark looked at Mikey and shouted, "Robin, call Cindy Brown and ask her to come over right away!" While Robin called Cindy, our neighbor and a nurse practitioner, Mark tried to pick Mikey up by the shoulders, but Mikey's body wouldn't bend. Mark then grabbed a phone and called Dr. Freund.

Cindy ran in and looked at Mikey. She tried to take his hand, but his arm wouldn't move. I saw Cindy's hand subtly move over her chest back and forth, up and down. It looked to me like she was quietly crossing herself. Cindy immediately agreed when Dr. Freund told us over the phone to meet him at Baptist Hospital right away. We hurriedly explained to Robin and Teddy that Mikey wasn't well and we were going to the hospital and Cindy would stay with them. Mark and I lifted Mikey together to get him to the car. Mikey was so stiff, I had to hold him across my lap in the backseat of the Honda Civic while Mark drove the five miles in the darkness of that mid-February evening.

Al Freund met us at the emergency room doors. He glanced at Mikey and said, "Oh shit."

Dr. Freund accompanied two people in scrubs as they put Mikey, still rigid, on a gurney and hurried off. Mark and I staggered, banging into the doors as we held each other and shook. I ran after Mikey's gurney. Mark joined me a few minutes later, explaining someone had led him to a cubicle where he filled out admittance paperwork. Mikey was in a private area of the emergency room. He was surrounded by doctors and nurses.

Mark and I stood at each side of his bed, each holding one of Mikey's hands. He looked relaxed now, no longer stiff. But the click of the ventilator dispelled any sense of normalcy. Just like eight years ago in the NICU, Mikey couldn't breathe on his own.

A neurologist came to speak with us. As she explained, I managed to hear sentence fragments through the roar of adrenaline in my ears. My left hand was in Mikey's, and my right was busy nervously spinning the teddy bear charm on my necklace.

"Pupils nonreactive…opisthotonic posturing…brainstem…possible aneurysm…not sure…bad…doll's eye test."

Al Freund stood at the foot of Mikey's bed.

"What, Doctor?" I asked the neurologist through the pounding noise in my head. Mark was holding my hand, his eyes tightly shut. Then he opened his eyes, blinked slowly, and looked at the wall next to the neurologist.

"What did you say about a doll's eye test and ice water?" Mark asked.

The doctor explained rapidly. Her voice was tight and high.

"I ran two tests so far, and the prognosis is poor. The first test was the doll's eye response, which evaluates brainstem function in patients who are unresponsive. A positive or normal reflex occurs when the eyes automatically move in the direction opposite to the rotation of the head. A negative response occurs when the eyes move in the same direction as the head rotation. That's what happened when I tested your son. This can mean severe brain damage or brain death. I also did a cold caloric test. In comatose patients with cerebral damage, this phase of nystagmus will be absent as it is controlled by the cerebrum. Using cold water irrigation results in deviation of the eyes toward the ear being irrigated. If both phases are absent, as in your son's case, this suggests the brainstem reflexes are also damaged."

Then she stopped talking. She looked at the floor for a long moment, then put her hand on Mark's shoulder, and looked me in the eye. My fingers loosened their grip on the teddy bear charm, and I felt it bang softly against my upper chest.

"I think your son is brain dead, Mr. and Mrs. Londner. I want to run one more test: a cerebral blood flow study. That will tell us for sure."

There was a moment of silence. Then Al Freund stepped forward and embraced us both.

"If he's not brain dead, then he is severely damaged. He'll never again be what he was." Freund's voice cracked, and his eyes filled with tears. "How could this happen?" he said softly, looking away from us.

Mark and I swayed together into an abyss. It was the old NICU question, only worse: What do we hope for now?

Mikey was wheeled away to undergo the final test. Mark and I waited in the hallway outside the testing area. I stared at the blue tiles along the wall. There was a series of little scratches on one of the tiles that looked like a dachshund. I tried to blank my mind, not knowing what to want. I flashed back to the NICU again. My thoughts there had been be well or be dead. Did I mean that? I stared at the tiled wall again. Now the scratches looked more like a short-legged cow. Maybe they just looked like scratches—like nothing.

Doors opened and the neurologist came out, followed by Mikey's gurney. She glanced at us quickly, bit her lower lip, and looked at us again, steadying her gaze. She shook her head and looked away again as she walked the gurney back to Mikey's alcove in the emergency room.

Dr. Freund followed last and came up to us. Mark and I were both slumped against the wall. "I am so sorry," he said. As he embraced us, he said, "I can't believe it."

Mark said, "What...what now?"

Freund took our hands, and we three walked together down the long, cold hallway.

"What now," he said, "is that we talk about organ donation."

I have a dreamlike memory of entering an office and sitting in a stiff wooden chair. Mark was sitting next me. There were papers—organ donation papers—in front of us. One of the questions asked if we wanted to be in contact with the recipient and family. We said yes.

Filling in the donation paperwork was physically difficult for me because of the tunnel vision I'd suddenly developed. Bile climbed into my throat as I thought of my child being surgically cut, yet again, this time for no benefit to himself. But I forced that primitive thought away. Others can live from our tragedy. My arm and fingers moved stiffly, but I signed the papers.

Our hands tightly clasped, Mark and I went into Mikey's room. He had been moved to a private room after the attempts in the emergency room to save his life failed. The room was huge, cold, and blue, and the adult-sized bed too big for such a little boy. His brain had died, but his chest moved up and down in perfect rhythm with the clicks of the ventilator that controlled the mechanical breaths. That breath nourished the organs we'd just signed away.

Mark and I sat on opposite edges of the bed, again, with Mikey between us, again. We held his hands and stroked his soft cheek and kissed him over and over. At the same moment, Mark and I each lay down and stretched out next to him. Mikey lay between us as we held him and each other. It was a ghostly echo of many a happy morning with a giggling boy laughing at our "Mikey sandwich" silliness.

I heard the voices of Robin and Teddy in the hallway. Cindy had driven them to the hospital. Dr. Freund must have called and suggested they come. Then I heard my parents and in-laws. Our rabbi's voice soon became distinct too.

"How are we going to tell them?" I asked Mark. The voices in the corridor got louder as our friends and family neared, bringing the reality of this nightmare with them with each approaching step.

"I don't know," he whispered to me as he stood to embrace his mother, who was stumbling into the room, crying. He glanced back at me as he reached out to steady her. "I don't know how to tell myself."

CHAPTER 26

Mikey's Funeral

I CLOSED MY EYES AND listened to Rabbi Rami Shapiro's prayers amid the sobs of my parents and in-laws and most of the other people there. The day before, my father, Mark, and I had stood together in the casket room of the Levitt Weinstein Memorial Cemetery for the surreal task of choosing a box and a place for our Mikey. We bought three cemetery plots—one for Mikey and one each for me and Mark on either side. Someday, the Mikey sandwich would be eternal. Now I opened my eyes and looked at the plain brown box in front of me.

Mark and I squeezed our hands together so hard that my palm ached for days afterward. My breath came in shallow huffs during much of the service, and I was lightheaded with grief and disbelief. I think I held Teddy, who was nearly six years old, in my arms, and I know Mark's other hand was holding tight to Robin's.

Through a haze of Hebrew, my thoughts returned to when Teddy and Robin had come in to Mikey's hospital room. Mark and I had stood up, each still holding one of Mikey's hands. We had thought we explained what had happened, but, evidently, we did a poor job. A few minutes later, Robin left the room to go to the bathroom. Dr. Freund spoke with her in the hallway. We heard the sound when she fell onto the carpet. She had hyperventilated and fainted once she understood her brother had died.

Teddy had seemed to understand, but when Cindy Brown's daughters gave him a handmade condolence card the next day, Teddy screamed at them.

"My brother's not dead!" he said. The girls started to cry. Teddy ran to Mark and me. He demanded, "Mikey is only sick. Tell me Mikey is only sick."

We tried to explain, again, gently. When Teddy realized the truth, he wouldn't look at us or talk to us for hours.

At the funeral, it was all hands. Hands and eyes. There were so many loving hands on me. So many eyes red and teary, like mine. Mark's fingers were stiff and dry, locked on mine. Orlynne, Mikey's beloved Sissy, sat behind me, her hand squeezing my shoulder with the rhythm of her sobs. Mari, my forever friend, was stroking my hair.

Many children from Mikey and Teddy's school were at the funeral: Mikey's second-grade classmates and Teddy's kindergarten friends. Some of Robin's sixth-grade friends were there. Teachers came too. The death of an eight-year-old is a shocking event.

When only Mark, Teddy, Robin, and I came home from the hospital after Mikey died, I had taken my clothes and teddy bear necklace off and threw them in a corner of my closet. I never wanted to see those clothes or that necklace again. They were the last things that touched me when I touched my son. I worried that, if I ever felt the cloth of the shirt or the dimples of the teddy bear's gold legs, I would never be able to feel anything else ever again.

Sitting at Mikey's funeral, I appreciated the stark honesty in Rabbi Rami's eulogy.

Rami said, "I have heard people say over the past several days that it doesn't matter how long a person lives; it is the quality of one's life that makes all the difference. While this is certainly true in the abstract, we must take care not to use it as a platitude, a cover-up, a shield that blinds us to the tragedy of our loss. There is a tragedy here that no talk of quality can rectify. Yes, there were eight years filled with much love and care. Yes, Mikey made of his eight years what few others could have made. Yes, with the love and help of his family, he overcame tremendous odds and was a real little mensch. And Mikey's life was too short."

Rami spoke of Mikey's love, his enthusiasm, his daring, his courage, his strength.

"You could see it in his eyes, in his face—he was a loving little boy," Rami said. "And, better still, you can see it in the eyes of everyone here. Mikey loved the people in his life. And, while people are most important, Mikey loved other things as well.

"Mikey loved to read; the bathroom was his private library. He loved Star Trek, so much that Robin would call him Spock. He loved to play bingo at Grandma's house. He loved his ever-improving ability to take care of himself, to master Spanish, to make the most of what he had. And most of all, he loved trains.

"This was Mikey's passion. He had his career mapped out: he wanted to be a Metrorail driver. He would talk about this with such insistence that Ronnie actually called Metrorail to find out how old a driver had to be. Eighteen is the minimum age, and when Mikey turned eight, he exclaimed with joy that he only had ten years to go before the job was his. And he would have made it too."

Rami said Mikey wove a tapestry of love, a blanket of courage and hope.

"He has left us in this tapestry the memories we carry and stories we share," Rami said. "Let his blanket warm you from the chill that haunts us at this moment. Wrap yourself in his love, and return it to others that his memory might be a blessing for all who knew him. Amen."

CHAPTER 27

Dr. Freund's Reaction

TWO WEEKS LATER, AL FREUND wrote out his thoughts as he, Mark, and I had walked together down the long, cold hallway of Mikey's death. I was astonished by his bravery, honesty, and compassion.

"He's brain dead."

The words struck like a torch searing through me just below my sternum. What did I do wrong? Why did this tragedy happen? Could I have overlooked something?

A flood of disorganized questions raced through my head and burned in my chest and stomach. Why do I always second-guess myself when something goes wrong?

I am angry, but I don't know where to direct the anger except internally. Somehow it seems incongruous that only ten to twelve hours ago, Michael was in my office joking even though he was in pain. How can I ever explain this tragedy to Mark and Ronnie and try to comfort them? Who is going to comfort me?

All the methods and words I have learned, over the past twenty-plus years of practicing pediatrics, to use to give solace and comfort to grieving parents at this moment sound like rationalizations.

It is now two weeks after the end of Michael Londner's abbreviated life. Michael truly lived. He surely suffered, gallantly gave, and finally lost.

I am still looking for answers. Perhaps life is like something Gertrude Stein once said, "There ain't no answer. There ain't going to be any answer. There never has been an answer. That's the answer."

CHAPTER 28

Reassuring Montessori Classmates

◦──∽──◦

Two or three weeks after the funeral, I went to Mikey's school. I sat on the floor in a circle with the twenty-five children from Mikey and Teddy's classes, kindergarten and second grade. Teddy sat on my lap. My goal was for the kids not to be afraid for themselves and not to think that people with disabilities like Mikey's were destined for a short life.

I looked around the room at the Children's House School. I was in the Practical Life section of this Montessori classroom, so I focused on the wooden baskets filled with tongs, tweezers, and basters. They were in the upper part of shiny white shelves. Baskets on the lower shelves held sponges, cloths, squeegees, and squirt bottles with a mixture of white vinegar and water. Mikey had taken pleasure in polishing and scrubbing, and he knew the joy of completing a task alongside his friends. He learned reading, arithmetic, and other core skills in this same gentle manner.

Mrs. Gomez signaled to me that the children were ready. I breathed in and began to tell them why their classmate and friend had died.

"I am here today to explain something important," I said. "I know you miss Mikey. You may have questions about the way he died. Mikey had an aneurysm. That means he had a weakened area in a blood vessel of his brain. No one knew about the weak area. Even if we had known, though, we couldn't have done anything about it."

A little girl sitting directly in front of me squirmed and held up her hand to ask a question. I smiled at her as tears stung my eyes; Carolina was one of Mikey's favorite classmates. They often had lunch together.

111

"How did he get the ander-ism?" Mrs. Gomez and I exchanged a glance at Carolina's endearing mispronunciation. "Could I have one too, or my sister?" Carolina asked. She leaned forward and scrunched the corduroy of her pants leg.

I told Carolina and the other children that the doctors think the aneurysm happened because of the brain injury Mikey had when he was born so early. As he grew, the weakened area in the blood vessel got bigger and finally burst.

"That didn't happen to you or your sister or anyone here," I told her. "And it doesn't happen to most people who are born early. It's very unusual."

Carolina sat back and her hand opened, relaxing her hold on her pants leg.

The children had a few more questions. Then some drew pictures of themselves with Mikey or of Mikey in heaven.

While they drew, I told the children that Mikey's heart and other organs were helping sick people to become well. These Montessori children knew all about recycling, and several nodded as we talked about organ donation. I asked Teddy if he wanted to draw with the other children, but he shook his head no and burrowed deeper in my lap.

My mind leaped from this vinegar-clean classroom to the antiseptic-clean hospital room where Mark and I lay alongside Mikey, listening to the click of the ventilator that kept his organs alive. His little chest moved up and down in perfect mechanical rhythm. But his brain—no. He was there and not there. I bit the inside of my lower lip, trying to use pain to bring me out of that horror and back to the classroom. I felt lost in despair and hoped I could make it through the rest of the visit with the children. I rested my head against Teddy's back. Then I realized that Carolina was standing next to me, a purple crayon still in her hand.

"Yes, sweetheart?" I asked, picking my head up.

"I just want to sit with you and Teddy for a minute, okay?" she asked.

Teddy looked up and moved from the center of my lap to my right leg. "You can have my mom's other leg," he told his friend. "The left one." I smiled, remembering listening in the hallway when Mikey taught Ted how to tell left from right.

Carolina carefully lowered herself onto my left knee. The children sat quietly for several minutes. I realized I wasn't lost in despair anymore. Instead, I was in excruciating pain from two kindergartners sitting on my legs. I laughed and hugged them both. They turned around and looked at me.

"I want to draw," said Teddy and stood up. My right leg throbbed.

"Let me show you my picture," said Carolina as she jumped up, giving my left leg a final burst of agony.

I couldn't move. I had to get on my hands and knees to finally stand up, but I blessed Carolina for taking me out myself and taking Teddy with her.

Then, suddenly, it was time for the children to resume their usual day. I said my good-byes to the children and Mrs. Gomez and walked stiffly to my car.

I opened the door and slid into the driver's seat. I put my head against the steering wheel and closed my eyes. I was emotionally drained but deeply grateful I had the opportunity to speak with the children.

That night, I was rummaging in the freezer for broccoli when I came across the frozen yogurt I'd gotten for Mikey the night before he died. His favorite. The plastic spoon was still in the cup, and little icicles had formed on the sides. I took it out of the freezer and groped for a chair. I sat, staring at the yogurt, at the spoon, at the cup. My hands became cold, but I couldn't let go. After a few minutes, I put the whole thing back into the freezer. I put the bag of frozen broccoli in front of it. I didn't want to see the yogurt, but I couldn't throw it away, either.

A few months later, Mark and I started a scholarship fund for children with disabilities at the Children's House. This was in response to the many people who asked where they could send a donation in Mikey's name. We were so pleased with the education, support, and fun Mikey had at the school, we decided to create a way to subsidize that for other children with disabilities whose parents could not afford it.

CHAPTER 29

A Prayer for Organ Donors

&

IN ONE OF A FEW follow-up calls from Jackson Memorial Hospital's transplant team, the director of education told me one of the reasons many people don't allow donation of their loved ones' organs is because they fear the process involved in taking the organs will interfere with the religious rituals that occur at a deathbed. Mark and I hadn't had that concern. But other people might feel easier about this heavy decision with a formal, religious seal of approval. I called Rabbi Rami and asked him to write a prayer for those about to make an organ donation.

Rami, who had stood with us at Mikey's deathbed, told me, "I feel like I've been waiting for this request." He immediately began work on the prayer. He called me later and said, "I felt it flow from me as if it had been there all along."

The prayer is, to the best of my knowledge, the only prayer of its type.

A Prayer for Those Making an Organ Donation

Each of us comes into this world
as a gift…bearing gifts…being gifts.
Each of us comes into this world
with a purpose…bearing meaning…being meaning.
Tell me—please!—why this suffering;
why this awful burden searing my heart
with a fire only love can survive…survive but not soothe.
There is no soothing in this pain:
No comfort in this loss;
No meaning in this mindless swirl of terror and tears.
There is only the numbing that accompanies
the ragged-edged hardness of life's too swift unfolding.
And yet the gift remains.
The moment shared and anticipated.
The dream lived and dreamt anew. The gift remains.
And with it the obligation—
making this world a little better for our having been here.
No matter how long or short the sojourn;
No matter even if the eyes never opened nor the lungs filled with air,
still the obligation remains.
How to meet it? We meet in death as we should meet it in life:
By giving the gift that each of us is.
By lending to others what has been lent to us: the gift of Life.
In the midst of our pain, we call out
to the One who establishes all things.
Feel my anguish as the decision is made.
Comfort me with the knowing that the way of this gift is the right way,
the way of compassion, the way of service, the way of caring, the way of Life.
Give me the courage to give the gift.
Grant me the strength to live with the giving.
Open my heart to the compassion

that knocks so softly at my soul's gate, whispering, "Give…"
To save a single life is to save an entire world.
May this world that is about to die embrace only peace.
May the world about to be saved embrace only love.
May the world that is about to be shattered know in time
The tender touch of healing.
The gift has been given. May it be for a blessing.
Amen.

CHAPTER 30

Grief

"Please let me know if there is anything I can do."

When Mikey died, people said that to me a lot. They brought food and thrust copies of *When Bad Things Happen to Good People* and *The Fall of Freddie the Leaf* at us. I knew they meant well, and we were grateful for their kindness. But we couldn't eat their food, and we couldn't read their books. My friend Mari, though, didn't ask what she could do. She just came over, day after day. Sometimes we didn't even speak; sometimes I didn't even see her. But she was there, doing laundry, cleaning dishes, mopping the floor, buying milk and eggs. Sometimes, she walked through my house crying, for she loved Mikey too. She might stay an hour or fifteen minutes. Some days she didn't come at all. But her love for me and my family trailed after her like a light perfume.

None of us could bear to enter the room where the boys had slept. Mark and I held our breath one day and brought out Teddy's dresser. We push-pulled it across the house to the room next to Robin's. That one-time guest room, too small for two boys, now would be for Teddy alone. It already had a bed, and it was only seven little Teddy-sized footsteps to Mark's and my bedroom. During many middles of the night, Robin and Teddy would separately find their way to our bed and we all slept—or cried—together.

One night, Robin had taken her shower and crawled under our comforter with her hair still soaking wet. Her blond hair was slicked back, and the water had darkened it to look brown. I walked out of the bathroom and, for an instant, I thought she was Mikey. There he was, with his brown hair gleaming on the pillowcase. She turned her head toward me, and my illusion vanished.

After Mikey died, our dog, Cleveland, kept looking for him. When Teddy would walk down the hallway, Clevie would peer expectantly behind him. Click-click-click, we'd hear her nails tapping on the tiled floor as she wandered the house. Nights were especially anxious for Cleveland. She roamed the house restlessly, going back and forth into the boys' former room at the other end of the house. She'd stand by Mikey's empty bed and sniff. She'd trot to the other end of the house to find Teddy, usually in our bed, and then hurry back to the bedroom the boys used to share. We all pet and hugged her over and over, but she clearly missed Mikey. Those two, canine and boy, had enjoyed a singular relationship. Because Mikey's preferred form of locomotion had been creeping on hands and knees, he was often at a level with the dog. Cleveland was a lovely, affectionate dog, greeting us all with a sweet wave of her tail. But when she approached Mikey, her tail wagged so powerfully she tilted from the effort.

One evening, about three weeks after Mikey died, Clevie stopped at his bed longer than usual. She sat down on her haunches, threw her head back, and howled. The howl rose in pitch and went on and on. I stared at her. My soul shook with the primitive and profound power of that howl. Suddenly, she stopped, shook herself, and trotted out of the room.

Her restless pacing ceased after that. Cleveland looked for Mikey no more.

Robin, meanwhile, wouldn't remove a big, gaudy purple ring from her finger. Dr. Freund had a wicker elephant goodie box filled with toys, stickers, and other little fun items kids could choose among when the medical visit was over. At his last appointment, Mikey chose a "ruby" ring from that toy basket especially for his sister.

A classmate asked Robin why she wore such an ugly ring. She told him, "Because my brother gave it to me."

The kid looked ashamed. He instantly apologized. His family attended our synagogue, and he knew what had happened.

"I felt bad for him," Robin explained to me. "But I didn't know how to apologize for him apologizing."

Both children were twelve years old.

After that, Robin turned the ring around so the gaudy part faced her palm. She told me she didn't want to draw attention to herself, but she still wanted Mikey's gift close to her.

The ring started out shiny, but it dulled. A crack developed, and then another. Robin wore it until it fell apart.

On subsequent visits to Dr. Freund's office, Robin saw the identical ring in the elephant basket, but she never chose it for herself.

On the verge of her teen years, Robin was just beginning to be interested in boys. But Mikey's death blindsided her. She turned inward.

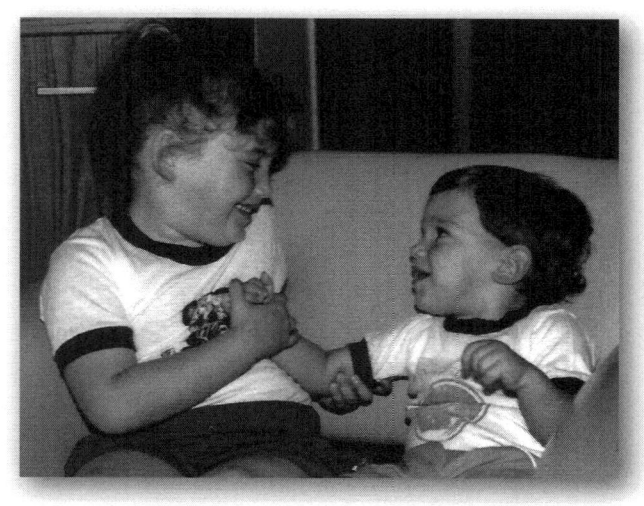

In some ways, Teddy's loss was the most profound. The boys had slept together, eaten together, went to school together, and often spoke in their own language. After his brother's death, Teddy had moments of anxiety and nervousness. One morning he said, "Mikey died, and it's like being lost in China and you can't find the other person forever."

He talked a lot and asked many questions. We answered the questions as best we could and encouraged more. We held him and held him.

Teddy started composing songs for Mikey. He'd sit on the piano bench, feet dangling high above the floor, and slowly play bass notes in a minor key. Mark and I would watch and listen, grateful for Teddy's expressive creativity. His compositions evolved and lengthened over the weeks and months, but always with a core of sad, low notes. He wrote about Mikey in the journal Montessori teachers assign their students, and he drew pictures. But the piano music—untaught, visceral, healing, and tragic—made me gasp.

Mark and I cried, together and apart. Many times, I cried with my father. "Daddy, the best years of my life are over," I once sobbed into his shoulder. He hugged me closer. I felt him take in breath, as if he was ready to argue with me or reassure me. But then he somehow hugged me even closer, and we sobbed together.

Mark and I scheduled some family trips. Perhaps we did it to forge new memories and get close to other family members. Perhaps we did it to get out of our house. Perhaps we did it just to have something to do. On one trip, we visited my brother's family in Oregon and my brother-in-law's in Washington state. We drove from San Francisco to Seattle via the Pacific Coast Highway. The pounding of the Pacific Ocean and the enormity of the old-growth redwood trees were soothing.

We took Robin and Teddy to England to visit family there. On a journey from Slough to London, I got separated from Mark and the kids when I took an earlier train by mistake. Mark and Robin fretted until we reunited at Paddington Station, but Teddy was frantic. Maybe he thought I had disappeared like his brother.

Simple, small talk questions like "How many kids do you have?" now gave me a dilemma and a stomachache. If I answered three, as I was used to doing, the follow-up "What are their ages?" twisted my guts even more. But it felt wrong to say two. It was as though I was denying Mikey ever lived. I handled the question differently depending on who was asking and why.

Having only two children was strange on many levels. Grief was overwhelming and constant. But I also had to adjust to the mundane, daily changes. I'd be food shopping and automatically toss Mikey's favorites in the cart—spaghetti, bread, and bananas. At the checkout line, I'd pull them off the conveyor belt and mumble to the cashier, "Sorry, I don't need this after all." Doing the laundry, I'd heft the basket and think, "Boy, that's light," and flash to knowing why. Setting the table for dinner, helping Teddy with his bath or homework, shopping for clothes, making school lunches—all were stabs of pain.

It used to always be a time-consuming project to take the three kids for frozen yogurt or similar outings. I'd have to carry Mikey and his wheelchair in and out of the car at home and at the yogurt shop. The first time I went out with Robin and Teddy after Mikey died, I thought how ridiculously easy it was. Tell the kids to get in the car, strap them in, and off you go. My God, so this is what it's like to have two able-bodied kids—how effortless.

Because Mikey nearly died so shortly after he was born, my fear of losing him simmered throughout his brief life. But expectation is intellectual. An empty bed is visceral. My family—my husband, my two sons, and my daughter—existed for just under six years.

Seven months after Mikey died, I wrote him a letter:

Dear Mikey,

The last time I wrote you a note it was for your lunch box. But now I can't make lunch for you anymore.

Mikey, I miss you so much. Even though I did everything I could to help you during your life, I feel like it is my fault you died. Sometimes I wish I died too. If I could have traded my life for yours, I think I would have, but I would have made a deal for you first.

The deal would be that you wouldn't be disabled and that your brother and sister would live long, healthy lives with you and that your father would remarry a nice woman so you could have a good stepmother. With those conditions, I think I would have given the rest of my life so you could have yours. But there was no one to make a deal with. And you died. And I hate it.

I need you, Mikey. You needed me during your life, and I didn't realize until now how much I need you. You were happy. You were sweet. You worked so hard. You made us all proud of you.

Sometimes you got angry at me, or the Bear or Rob, but that is how families are. You didn't hold a grudge. You tried hard to lose weight, because you knew it was difficult for Papa or me to carry you. But when we did carry you, you always kissed us and hugged us so lovingly. You were a grateful child.

You used to fall asleep so quickly. I remember how you'd fall asleep in the van coming home from your grandparents' house, and then you'd get so mad when we'd arrive home and shut off the engine. That woke you up, and you'd yell that we should keep driving. But after Papa carried you in, and I stripped off your clothes and put you in a nightshirt, you'd snuggle into the pillow and smile.

You and the Bear slept together every night and made each other safe. If I win the Nobel Prize for finding the cure for cancer, or the Pulitzer Prize for writing the best article on whatever, I am still a failure. The most important thing is for me to help you. I helped you for eight years, but then you died. I couldn't help you live. I didn't know what to do to make you live and be well. Maybe nothing would have helped, but that doesn't matter; I didn't help you, so I failed in the most important mission of my life. Sometimes I want to lie down and die, because I failed you.

Oh, my 'Cro. I remember your happy face when you'd bring home a spelling test with "100 percent" on it. And you did that many, many times. You'd tell Papa about your test, and he'd be so proud, and you'd get a poke in the belly that would make you laugh so hard you'd fall over. So proud of you, 'Cro.

You would have, should have, been nine years old tomorrow. You were planning a slumber party. You wanted to invite Teddy and Mutti and Daddy.

Pop and I would sing and play with you—
Michael D.
Boy for me.
Sweetest guy in all the world.
Bar none.
Then we'd each hold one of your arms and play-fight over you—
My boy.
No, my boy.
No, *my* boy.
No, my boy.
Then we'd both hug you and say,
"Okay—we share."

You always loved that game.

I am so angry you died. You—and we—tried so hard. But Mikey, I am so glad you lived. We only had you with us for eight years and five months, and I am glad, so glad, you lived and flourished for that time.

Love,
Mama

CHAPTER 31

The Visit

Sleep came in trickles, and I'd awaken exhausted as the reality hit me. I couldn't hold Mikey anymore. I couldn't put my face next to his silky cheek, couldn't smell his sweet little boy smell, couldn't see his hazel eyes up close, and couldn't feel his warm breath on my neck.

I would slip out of bed, careful not to disturb Mark's restless sleep, and roam the house. I'd check on the other children. I'd stroke their cheeks as they slept, and I'd rearrange their bedcovers. I'd go into the living room and sit on the rug next to Cleveland. She would look at me and put her head in my lap. I'd stroke her too.

But I'm not a parched soul in the desert where any liquid—however precious—will do. I must have one particular water of life, one particular cheek to stroke and brow to kiss. I'd get off the floor and go back to bed, thirsty still, thirsty forever, and hope I'd dream of him and stroke his face in my sleep.

Then one night, it happened.

Mikey visited me and gave me what I craved. It was more than a dream; it was a visit. Mikey, himself, came to me. He knew that I needed to understand that he still existed in some form.

In the dream, I am driving the van. Robin sits next to me, and Teddy is behind me. We drive along. The children are talking. Suddenly, I hear Mikey's voice. We all turn around to the direction of his voice, and we see him in his usual spot, sitting behind Robin.

"Mikey!" we scream together, delighted. We all speak at once, excited to see him.

"Hi, guys," he says. "How have you been?"

We realize we have made a ridiculous mistake; of course he is not dead. I drive along for a while, continuing toward our destination. I drive through a pleasant small town passing storefronts and people strolling along the sidewalk. It is sunny and soothingly warm—a lovely day. I have my children; I am happy.

I drive a little further and notice an open space ahead and to my left. I see the ocean and a sandy beach. I realize this is our destination. I pull over to the side of the road in this sweet little town and turn off the engine.

I remember something and turn to my daughter. "Rob, " I say, "did we remember to bring the wheelchair?"

Rob replies, "No, Mama, we didn't."

I turn apologetically to Mikey and say, "Sweetie, I am so sorry, but we've gotten out of the habit of bringing the wheelchair in the van, and we don't have it."

Mikey smiles, and says, "Don't worry, Mama. I don't need it. You can carry me."

I smile back at him, feeling relieved. "Of course I can."

I get out of the van and slam the door behind myself. I'm careful, because the traffic is coming against me. The air is full and balmy with the invigorating, salty tang of the ocean. I take a deep breath and walk around to the other side of the van.

I open the front door. Robin hops out. I pull the handle on the long side door that opens to the rest of the van. Teddy scrambles out, and Mikey grins at me, releases his seat belt, and extends his arms to me. His right arm is fully extended, the left only partially so. Within the dream, I realize this is more than a dream—this is somehow real, or partly real.

I breathe deeply again, savoring the briny air that is somehow central to the dream. I put out my arms, and Mikey throws himself into my embrace. I hold him and smell his hair. I am content. The ache, the torment of not holding him, is gone.

Then I realize, this can't be Mikey—he is too light. I braced my body for his fling into my arms, and the weight never hit me. It can't be 'Cro; he was never light, gossamer, ephemeral. I feel uneasy, nervous, and betrayed. Automatically, as I've done hundreds of times, I shift him onto my right hip. As I do so, I touch and hold his bare feet. His feet! They are soft and tender, as only Mikey's feet can be.

This isn't a dream; it is real, or real-ish. These feet that walked so seldom and kept their baby softness—they are real. I can almost feel the freckle on the bottom of his left foot. My unease is gone, and the craving for him is fulfilled again. I put my cheek against his, and his arms go around me. I am blissful, and I feel his bliss at our body-and-soul reconnection. I breathe deeply, and the ocean air fills my lungs. I pull Mikey tighter to me as he wraps his arms around my neck. Somehow, in the dream, I hold Mikey and also grasp the hands of Robin and Teddy.

Together, we carefully, cautiously, cross the street toward the strip of sand and ocean. I know that as we get closer to the beach, it will be larger, until it fills our world. It is peace; it is freshness; it is renewal. I have all my children; I am complete.

The alarm clock goes off, and I am jolted away. I am in my bed; Mark is next to me, and I am sobbing. Mikey is dead again. I cannot smell the ocean. I cannot feel my son's arms around me. But still, he was there with me. Mark reaches for me, startled and concerned. My sobs ease, and I confuse my poor husband by smiling at him as the tears roll down my cheeks. I feel the reality change but not fade away.

Mikey visited me.

CHAPTER 32

Corresponding with Organ Recipients

IN EARLY MARCH, ABOUT TWO weeks after Mikey died, we got a thank-you letter from the hospital transplantation department. It said:

> On the 17th of February, 1990, you were considerate enough to offer the transplantable organs from your son, Michael. I am pleased to inform you that transplantation has been performed…The right kidney was transplanted to a twenty-nine-year-old man, and the left kidney was transplanted to a thirty-year-old man…Both recipients are doing well and expected to be discharged in the near future. In addition, Michael's heart was transplanted to a seven-year-old boy… and his liver was transplanted to a four-year-old boy…Patients are recovering and doing well.
>
> Because of your generosity, these patients, who have had to depend on the artificial kidney machine, will now be able to continue to live normal lives. The children who received Michael's heart and liver now have a chance to become productive adults; without Michael's gift that would not be possible.

I was home alone, reading those words over and over: "considerate enough to offer the transplantable organs from your son," "recipients are doing well," "children who received Michael's heart and liver," "Michael's gift." Mark was at work, and Robin and Teddy were at school. I walked and thought in circles around the house. I read the letter again, I held it to my stomach, I read the letter again, and I held it to my chest. I was oblivious to what room I was in and where I was going. This letter was a link to my son. Wasn't it? My thoughts were a jumble. "My baby. In other babies. Other people. How awful. How wonderful. If he can't be—let them be. I want Mikey to be. I need him."

I blindly stepped on Cleveland's paw. She had been sleeping in the living room, but now she yelped in pain. I snapped out of my trance when I heard her cry and sat on the floor next to her to apologize. I folded up the letter and put it on the floor next to me. As I petted and kissed Cleveland's sleek head over and over, I wondered if we would receive any letters from recipients and if I would answer if we did. I thought about what the transplant coordinator told us when we signed the paperwork.

There were complex rules governing contact. We couldn't just write a letter and send it directly to the recipient. Recipients could not write directly to us. Correspondence had to be conveyed through the two hospitals involved.

If we wished to write, we had to address our letter in a generic manner, such as "heart recipient," and mail it to the transplant department at the Miami hospital. From there, our letter would be sent to the hospital where the recipient received the organ. Then that hospital would forward our letter. In the case of a child, our letter would be sent to the family.

This process could take weeks, if not months. The transplant coordinator told us our letters might be read along the way by hospital officials. This was to ensure we followed the rules to avoid writing anything that would identify us or where we lived. Such information would be censored. This made sense to Mark and me. We understood people might wish to protect their privacy. We did not initiate correspondence with any of the recipients. When I showed Mark the letter from the transplant hospital showing there were four people alive and thriving because of Mikey, his mouth smiled, but I heard the choke in his throat.

"Do you want to write to any of them?" I asked Mark.

"No," he said. "I can't. I just can't."

On December 19, 1990—nine years to the day that we took Mikey home from the NICU and also our fourteenth wedding anniversary—we received another letter from the transplant department. This letter looked different; it was in a bigger, bulkier envelope. I sat the envelope on the dining room table and looked at it. My hands shook a little as I opened it.

There was a cover letter in front of what felt like lots of folded papers. The cover letter stated, "I am sending you a letter sent to me from the family of the child who received Michael's heart. I sincerely hope their gratefulness to you will bring a measure of comfort to you."

I put the sheet of paper on the table and reached inside the envelope. My shaky hands made me clumsy. Envelopes spilled on the floor. I carefully slid off my chair, sat on the floor next to them, and reached for the nearest. Inside that envelope was another. I opened that one and finally unfolded a letter on five-by-seven-inch white, lined notebook paper. The words on it were written in a child's careful, bulky block letters, with a soft pencil and no erasures. I held the paper to my chest, thinking of the heart that beat while those little fingers held the pencil that formed the words. I brought the letter in front of my blurred eyes and read.

> Dear Donor's Mom + Dad
>
> Tuesday I am going to be in a Christmas play and I'm going to be a grasshopper. And I got my gradecard two months ago and I got all A's on my gradecard. I just got a check up and everything is fine. I am playing football at school with my friends outside. I am going to be in basketball. A friend and I rode in a bikeathon and rode ten miles. I go for my next check up in two months. Thanks for everything. Got to go. Merry Christmas. Also at night when we go to bed we pray for the little angel on this card who is your son. I am going to write JoAnne now to see if she will come and play a game.
>
> Love,
>
> Me

I folded the letter back into thirds. I put it in my shirt, patted it, and opened the next envelope. It contained a Christmas card with an angel on the front. Inside the card was another letter. This one was also on lined notebook paper folded in thirds. The penmanship was beautiful, 1950s cursive—open, looped, and easy on the eyes. I held this letter to my chest also and, closing my eyes, felt kindness and friendliness surround me. Still sitting on the floor, I leaned against a table leg and read.

> Dear Donor Family,
> As Thanksgiving and the holiday season approach, we remember the things we are thankful for. We just want you to know we are so very thankful for you. You have given one of the best gifts—the gift of life…
> Our son is in the third grade and doing super. His teacher says there are no problems. We'll know for sure because Friday is gradecard day. Ha. He plays tackle football and basketball. He passed swimming lessons this summer and rode ten miles in a bikeathon… He plays third base in Little League. The first game he hit two home runs. Everyone in the bleachers gave him a standing ovation…When we go to bed at night, we still say a prayer for Jesus to bless your little angel in Heaven who shared his heart. Together our sons are a team because your child lives on through ours.
> Feel free to write to us when that notion strikes. You will forever hold a special place in all our hearts. And remember we love you. May God bless you with a very blessed holiday season.
> Love from Your Unknown Friends

The letters were written before Thanksgiving and arrived a few days before Christmas. But here they were, now, in my hand. I had no doubt I would answer them.

It was a mother-to-mother correspondence for the most part, although Mark eagerly read her letters too. Over the next many months, the letters revealed the boy's mother to be a loving, gracious woman, Christian, and ever grateful to us for the heart that saved her son's life. I didn't always agree with her "everything happens for a reason" philosophy—it's harder from the donor perspective—but I admired her willingness to stay in touch. I think many mothers in her position would rather think of the heart that saved her son's life as a medical device, not an organ that belonged to a child conceived in love that grew beneath another woman's heart.

Getting to the letter was always an exercise in Russian dolls. Each hospital used its own envelope, so I had to open a large envelope to find a smaller one, then a still-smaller one, then at last the prize—a letter from the woman who could put her head on her son's chest and hear my son's heartbeat. The boy continued to write often too, telling tales of school, siblings, grandparents, football, and baseball. His world was health and life.

We heard once from the liver recipient, and we heard twice from one of the kidney recipients. They were kindly thank-you notes, and Mark and I appreciated them. But our heart-family, as I began to think of them, were different.

I looked forward to the letters and answered them quickly. But a part of me dreaded their arrival too. The dull ache I swam in all day every day sharpened to anguish when I touched the paper that came from the house where my son's heart now lived.

CHAPTER 33

Grief's Unveiling

Eleven months after Mikey died, Mark and I followed Jewish tradition and held an unveiling. At the ceremony meant to denote the end to formal grieving, the cemetery marker is "unveiled." For Mikey, we had chosen a simple, granite marker with a small train. The words gave Mikey's birth and death dates and also said: "A brave and loving boy."

Family and friends stood with us by the graveside as I thanked them for their love during Mikey's life.

Over the next weeks and months, the cemetery became familiar to me, as Teddy often asked to come. He would sit by Mikey's grave and play. Robin would refuse to come out of the car. I would stand there, among all my children.

For about a year after Mikey died, I cowered in my ravine of grief. I did my work, I cared for Robin and Teddy, and I went about my life in a superficial way. Mark and I talked about our mutual fog.

"It's a relief to go to work," he confessed. "It's a bit of a distraction to deal with Miami's drug murders, immigration battles, and government corruption."

I cried often—huge, wracking sobs that made me feel sick to my stomach. Tears brought no relief, but they flowed nonetheless. My health and fitness deteriorated. As a child, I had been a dedicated tomboy. I loved climbing trees, playing kickball or stickball in the street, and riding horses. Since becoming a mother, the most exercise I got was sporadic aerobics classes and marathon diaper changes.

In my stupor of grief, I did even less. I got pneumonia because I ignored a bad cough. I lost weight and then gained it. I tired easily. I'd go into a room and forget why I was there. My freelance writing and research work became a struggle because my creativity and thinking skills fell apart.

Nearly two years after Mikey died, the anguish of my ongoing sorrow continued to come in waves. Sometimes, with great effort, I could swim with my head above water. Other times I was knocked down by despair and drowned for a while.

Sometimes I tortured myself by listening to the audiotapes I'd made of the kids playing. Our family of journalists, teachers, and writers is made of inveterate note takers and chroniclers. Like most families, we made videos of birthday parties and other special events, but I also made audio recordings of moments in an ordinary day. When I listened to recordings of the boys playing together, I would get intensely jealous of myself. I hear Mikey call me, "Mama! Can I have some juice?" I answer in a voice that is further away than Mikey's because he's in the playroom and I'm in the kitchen: "In a sec!"

I'm furious with myself in the tape for not responding immediately—I want to scream to that self, "Get him the juice! He's thirsty!"

I know it's ridiculous. I listen to his sweet voice, playing with his brother Teddy, pretending to be trains, listening to music, singing songs. The audio recordings engender an intimacy more intense than video. With video I am an observer. But listening, with my eyes shut, I am there.

He calls again, "Mama! Come here for a second!" I hear myself answer from the kitchen, "Coming!" My voice gets closer and clearer, and I say, "Yes, dear love?" Mikey asks for something; I answer. I am so jealous of that woman in the tape, talking with precious Mikey so casually, as though he'll always be there.

Mark and I went for counseling sessions on and off. The psychologist, Doris Stiles Glazer, knew me well. She had been one of my professors when I was studying for my master's degree in counseling psychology. Mark and I also had seen her professionally a few times after Mikey's difficult beginning. Doris was supportive, insightful, and generous with her time and caring.

I knew it was ludicrous to blame myself for Mikey's death, but sometimes I grew dizzy as I hyperventilated, believing I should have somehow done something to prevent his early birth and death. As his mother, I felt responsible for everything that happened to my child. The counseling was helpful, but I couldn't get past a certain point in the rumination of my grief. I needed to move—literally and figuratively—from anguish to action. I needed to get out of my head.

I started doing step aerobics again. That helped a bit. At the urging of my wise forever-friend Mari, I joined a yoga class. It was a revelation. On the car ride home from the first class, I cried the whole drive. Those tears were healing tears. The stretching and tensing in class released some of the grief that had been trapped for so long.

I started going to yoga two or three times a week. Sometimes, during the relaxation period at the end of class, I felt my body drift away. I could mentally touch Mikey then and feel his soft cheek against mine.

About six months into yoga, I joined a women's baseball league. No one else volunteered for catcher, so I took it on and found I loved the aggressiveness of that position. When I caught a foul pop-up or stood at home plate with the ball in my mitt waiting for the runner to come in from third base, I was in the moment. I was there, with my grief pushed aside for that instant.

My body felt alive again, and I longed to feel life inside me. I wanted to have another baby. I was 43. Mark was nervous.

"Oh my God, Ron, are you sure you want to do this?" he asked me when I brought up the topic of pregnancy over and over again

On Dr. Hanft's advice, we consulted with a high-risk specialist at the University of Miami medical school's department of obstetrics. After examining me and my medical records, Dr. Lee gave us the go-ahead to try for another baby. As we got into the elevator for the ride down from the doctor's office, I saw Mark appeared to be chewing on the inside of his cheek.

"How do you feel about what the doctor said?" I asked him.

He was silent during the descent. As the elevator doors opened, he turned to me and answered. "I've been thinking about how to describe it. Maybe there's a word in German for it—it has a great vocabulary for complicated feelings. The closest I can get is joyful and terrified."

It had always been easy for me to conceive, and in a few months we were back at Dr. Lee's office. Dr. Hanft had already confirmed my pregnancy.

Dr. Lee was charmingly enthusiastic as he greeted Mark and me. He knew my medical history, of course, and of Mikey's death. I could feel his eagerness for our happiness.

"You are about six weeks," he said, after the exam and test results. "Everything looks perfect."

As we prepared to leave his office, he stood and shook Mark's hand. Then he turned to me and grasped my hand with both of his.

"Smooth as silk!" he said, with gusto. "That's my hope and expectation for this pregnancy—smooth as silk!"

This time Mark and I laughed the whole way down in the elevator, repeating to each other, "Smooth as silk!"

I continued to feel well and Mark continued to worry, but we were both cautiously delighted.

When I went to Dr. Hanft's office for my three-month checkup, I got a lovely surprise from the office staff. As I walked in, the nurse, the receptionist, and the bookkeeper stood up and began chanting my name:

"Ron-nee, Ron-nee, Ron-nee!"

Some of the other patients in the waiting room picked it up and began chanting too. They couldn't have had any idea what it was about, but it was heartwarming. I felt like a football hero, carrying my slightly swollen belly. I was a new version of happy. I was living around the chasm in my heart, like a tree with a great wound.

Dr. Hanft checked me over. Everything was perfect. I was basking in creation and growth.

CHAPTER 34

Smelling the Storm

THE PUBLIC SERVICE ANNOUNCEMENT MARK and I had made about organ donation was in heavy rotation on WSVN. Sometimes, it came on the air just before Mark had to report his story for the day. As he ran through his thirty-second countdown before going on the air, Mark would have to watch the PSA's video of himself and me discussing our decision to donate Mikey's organs. The PSA ended with a clip we had given the PSA's editor of Mikey up front on the monorail ride at Disney World.

"It's hard to start my stand-up about the bozos at City Hall or whatever nonsense is happening that day when I've just seen my precious boy on the monitor. But I can never look away," Mark said.

The PSA bothered Mark so much, he asked me how I would feel if he asked the station to pull it off the air. Then WSVN got a letter. A family wrote to tell how they gathered in their relative's hospital room. The young man was brain-dead. His parents refused when doctors asked about organ donation. But the grandmother had something to say.

"Remember how Mark Londner donated his son's organs?" the grandmother had said. "He saved lives. We should too."

The family donated the organs.

When Mark brought home that letter, we agreed not only to keep the PSA on the air, but we also made a second PSA. I was nearly fourteen weeks pregnant when we made that one. My little belly was not visible, but my hair was glossy and my fingernails long—both of which are sure signs of pregnancy for me.

Soon after making the second public service announcement, WSVN assigned Mark to cover the coming hurricane. It was late August 1992. He hated leaving me, Robin, Teddy, and Cleveland alone in the house, but his job demanded it. Hurricane Andrew was predicted to make landfall about thirty miles north of our neighborhood. That didn't sound too bad. So off he went, looking back at me and saying, "Sorry. This sucks."

By midnight, the predictions for landfall veered south and included our zip code.

By 2:00 a.m., my hands were damp and my heart beat in my throat as I listened to the rising storm and contemplated being alone with my children. I needed to be strong for them, but as the winds strengthened, I felt weak. How could I protect my children, my pregnancy, and myself?

For maximum safety, the hurricane pundits advised hunkering down in a closet centrally located in the house. Following their advice, the kids, dog, and I crunched into the forty-two-inch by fifty-two-inch linen closet. We leaned against cases of toilet paper, amid the smells of soap, towels, and sheets. We rolled Teddy's fish tank into the bathroom across from the closet and fed the two blue-neon guppies. They were the only ones who had appetites.

At 2:45 a.m., I heard a pounding at the front door. At first I thought it was tree branches, but the dog jumped up from her spot with us in the closet and ran to the door, barking. "Cleveland, no, come back!" I called. Then the yelling began.

"Move the stuff, and let me in!"

It was Mark.

I struggled to get to my feet and out of the linen closet. I ran to the front door and scrambled to move the chairs, desk, and boxes we'd put against the door in an effort to keep Andrew on the other side. I finally cleared the area and wrenched the door open, staggering backward as the vortex of wind slammed and swirled. I caught a glimpse of bent-over trees as Mark bounded in. Together, we pushed the door shut again. He restacked our pile of protection against the door as Cleveland barked, jumped, and licked Mark's hand. Robin and Teddy added to the clamor.

"I had to come home when they changed the landfall," he said as he squeezed into the linen closet with me and the children. Cleveland curled up in her spot again next to the case of toilet paper.

At 4:30 a.m., lights flickered and then stayed off. They wouldn't come back on for nearly a month. We saw nothing beyond flashlight range, but we heard and smelled and felt the storm. Branches began cracking, and then came the deeper, never-before-heard sound of trees splitting apart. The wind flew around the house like a dervish trying to get in. I suddenly understood why hurricanes have names; the wind seemed a demon spirit. A sound like machine-gun fire beat against the windows in the two east-facing bedrooms down the hall. The windows burst, and the dervish was in our bedrooms, smashing and howling and exploding.

Robin cried out, "My ears!" My ears popped too, and I felt an unnatural lurch in my three-and-a-half-months pregnant womb.

We held each other as the winds roared around the house. We heard pieces of roof pull off with tearing, grinding noises and then whoosh as they flew away. Water seeped in from the east side of the house and spread to the hallways and beyond. The brackish water was rain made of seawater. As it came into our closet, we stood or crouched to keep from sitting in the wet. We waited for the eye—the eye of the hurricane that would bring momentary silence.

Suddenly, it was there. Quiet. We steeled ourselves for the blink of the eye and the return of the storm on the other side. The silence stretched. I threw every towel and sheet on the floor so we could sit. We collapsed on the temporarily dry linen and waited.

One by one, the others fell asleep. Cleveland and I were the only ones awake. I stroked her smooth head until she fell asleep too. Andrew was gone, swirling south for Homestead. We later learned we had been in the eye wall and therefore spared a second strike. However, the eye wall produces a storm's most damaging winds and intense rainfall.

At 8:30 a.m., we stirred and emerged from the closet, walking stiffly. We decided the winds had died down enough to venture outside. We moved the furniture stacked against the front door and stepped over the threshold. We were aliens on our own planet. The stomach-churning smell of exploded trees mixed with the swampy odor of salty rain. We were in an estuary of warped metal, broken houses, and uprooted, defoliated trees. We could not get past the front door. Our prolific grapefruit tree, grown from seed years ago by Mark's grandmother, lay twisted and split on our front walk. Tiny, immature grapefruits lay scattered about.

It was still raining, and the streets were empty.

Suddenly, an apparition in a yellow slicker appeared. It was Phil Gobie from across the street. He was going door to door, checking on every neighbor. He knew I was pregnant and came to check on me first. He smiled when he saw Mark with me on the threshold. Phil waved with his flashlight and, through the fog of rain, moved on down the block.

There were no air conditioner compressors powering on, no cars or buses, no kids yelling, no dogs barking, no birds calling out their morning songs. The only sound was of the now-gentle, steady rain.

But, in two days, the noise in the neighborhood became nearly unbearable. There was a constant barrage of chain saws, generators, and helicopters. In front of every house was a growing mountain of rotting trees, soaked carpets, and ruined furniture. We found a confused-looking small shark in our now-greenish swimming pool. We saw and smelled columns of yellow-brown smoke from a nearby emergency trash burning center. The inside of our house stank with fuzzy or slimy mold and mildew—black, green, brownish red, and even blue.

We had no running water because we were on wells that drew their water by electricity. We used pool water to flush the toilets, which we did sparingly. I longed for a shower and a cool breeze.

Every neighbor's home was severely damaged. An unbroken window was rare, and an intact roof was extinct. Hopeful people spray-painted the name of their homeowners insurance company across the front of their homes. No one had phone service or any other way to contact the outside world. The Herculean task of cleanup daunted us all. Where to begin? Everything needed doing at once.

Bob, our across-the-street neighbor, raked his front yard, slowly, quietly and meditatively.

The other Bob, down the street, focused on pulling soggy carpet out of his house, piling up mounds of rapidly molding rugs and foam mats.

Mrs. Bryan walked about in her nightgown that first day, shaking her head as she circled her house. Mr. Bryan sat inside next to some of his broken windows and called out, "They're so clean, it's like they're not even there."

Joanne, from down the street, and Cindy, from across the street, became the two-woman swimming pool cleanup team. They went from house to house with nets and brushes. Among the flotsam they fished out from the neighborhood pools were branches, roof tiles, a tricycle, that confused shark, frogs, and a cast-iron hibachi. Bob took the little shark to nearby Biscayne Bay; the frogs were on their own.

We all sorely missed the modern conveniences, especially electricity. But there were compensations: At night, we neighbors often found each other outside, basking in the glorious, deep darkness that gave us the stars in a way previously unseen from our suburban lawns. We had communal dinners, putting our canned goods together and cooking on the rescued hibachi. We entertained ourselves playing Spoons or card games.

The wildlife became even wilder. We saw cherry-head parrots and green-wing macaws—escapees from nearby Parrot Jungle. We saw iguanas, Cuban lizards, huge toads, and the occasional turtle. But less pleasantly, we also had to contend with rats in the growing piles of yard waste. Many of the heaps of branches stretched five feet high, and they lined the street on both sides. Chunks of pink fiberglass roof insulation dotted our lawns and scratched our throats.

Then the mosquitoes came, bred from the stagnant water. The buzzing and biting were maddening. Children and adults scratched and cried. We tried to hide indoors at dawn and dusk, the worst times. Two days passed, and, while standing with Bob and Cindy on their front lawn, we heard the drone of C-170 airplane engines roaring louder than the mosquitoes. We looked up and saw a contrail of droplets spreading out and drifting down.

"I can't breathe that; I'm pregnant!" I suddenly thought and began running. I was more afraid of the poison than of the mosquitoes.

"Where are you running to, Ron?" Bob called out as I crossed his lawn. The plane puttered on overhead, blanketing the area.

I stopped short and looked back at him. "I don't know," I replied slowly, realizing the futility. I turned and walked to my ruined house, trying to hold my breath.

I was getting worried about my pregnancy for other reasons too. Before the storm, I had felt the butterfly wings of fetal quickening. Now, two weeks after Andrew, nothing. I had to get to Dr. Hanft.

But we were isolated by the lack of phone service and electricity. Mark hadn't gone back to work yet. Our cars were damaged by fallen trees, but the little Honda Civic was operational. We decided to take a chance that Hanft's office would be open. It felt strange getting into the car again. We left Robin and Teddy with Bob and Cindy Brown, and Mark drove me to Dr. Hanft's office, a few miles north of our neighborhood and a bit less devastated.

We were lucky. Dr. Hanft was at his office, and he greeted us warmly. He was about to go see patients at South Miami Hospital, and he suggested Mark and I go with him so he could do an ultrasound there. We followed him.

The atmosphere at the hospital was storm-casual—a "we're in this together" attitude between staff and patients that was refreshing. The hospital was running on generators, and it took a while to find a room with a working sonogram machine. Dr. Hanft did the ultrasound himself, squeezing the cold jelly on my belly and pressing the wand down. Mark held my hand. We all stared at the monitor. Nothing. Hanft tried every angle on my belly, over and over. Nothing. My fear realized, a grinding pain began in my womb.

"I'm sorry, Ronnie. I'm sorry, Mark," Hanft said. His face was gray.

"It was Andrew, wasn't it?" I asked, remembering the lurch I felt when the barometric pressure plummeted.

"Oh, no, the storm probably had nothing to do with it. You're over forty, and there might have been something wrong with the baby," Hanft replied.

"Bullshit," I thought. Then I sat up on the examining table, jelly oozing onto my pulled-down maternity pants. We hadn't bothered with niceties like paper gowns.

Hanft was explaining that he'd have to do a D & C (dilation and curettage) on me to remove the "detritus."

"Will you please, please, do a karyotype? I need to know," I insisted.

I knew a karyotype test would show if there were abnormal chromosomes. Dr. Hanft agreed and scheduled me for the D & C in a few days. With the disruption of the hurricane, it could not be done immediately. Mark and I went home with the dead fetus inside me. I was too stunned to cry.

CHAPTER 35

Fishing for Life

THE NEXT DAY I DRIFTED about the house and yard, aimlessly picking up hurricane debris. I paused in front of the fish tank, restored from the bathroom back to its rightful place in the living room. I stared at the guppies. They used to flash about the crystal-clear tank like streaks of blue lightning. But their water was murky yellow now, and they seemed to trudge. I decided to worry about them.

"Mark, don't you think the fish look depressed?" I went outside to ask my husband. He and the children were bustling about the yard, filling huge contractor trash bags with the roof shingles, tree branches, and pink patches of roof insulation that littered the lawn.

They all came in the house and gathered around the fish tank.

Teddy piped up first. "Are the fish okay?"

Robin delivered her verdict: "They look sick."

Mark shook his head and glanced at me over the children's heads. "They're fine," he said. "Why don't you lie down?" He began to head outside again. "C'mon, kids."

"Wait!" I said. "I think I know what's wrong. It's the water."

We still had plenty of fish food, but we hadn't filtered or changed their water since there was no clean water to be had. We couldn't do anything to speed restoration of electric service to power our well water, so I decided it was imperative to get fresh water for the fish.

"Let's go to the Douchas!" I declared. "They have the great luxuries—water and electricity."

Mark knew he was beaten, so he abandoned the trash bags and picked up two empty buckets, and we all headed north to South Miami in the storm-battered little Honda.

We returned an hour later with two brimming buckets of fresh Doucha water. I netted the fish and put them in a temporary bowl with the old water while Mark and Robin replaced the tank water. We put the fish back in the now-clean, clear aquarium. I fed the fish and, after a dinner of canned beans, we all went to sleep in the stifling-hot house.

"Job well done," I thought. "We saved two lives today."

In the morning I woke early and went straight to the living room to check on the guppies. When I saw them both floating belly-up, I was bewildered. I wrenched open the front door and stumbled outside. I was on the verge of hysteria, and I didn't want to wake my sleeping family. I stood on the front lawn next to the twisted remains of our mailbox.

What happened? What went wrong? I moaned as the realization hit me that the Douchas' city water was treated. It had chlorine. Our well water came straight up through the ground and did not. I killed the guppies with kind intentions, profound ignorance, and bad water. Bob and Cindy were already outside on cleanup duty. They looked across the street at me, standing in my nightie, groaning. They knew I had miscarried and was scheduled for the D & C.

"What is it, Ron?" Cindy called out, ever a nurse. "Are you all right?"

"I can't keep anything alive," I said to the Browns, bursting into tears. "The fish are dead."

Cindy and Bob dropped their rakes and crossed the street. They both embraced me. They knew before I did that while I was crying about the guppies I was also finally sobbing for the little fish floating belly-up in my own belly.

When the dilation and curettage was over a few days later, Mark took me and the children to my parents' intact house nearly fifty miles north. It was clean and cool there.

A few days after that, we got the karyotype report from the hospital: a normal little girl, chromosomally perfect. And I was empty, my scraped womb weeping red onto a supersized Kotex.

CHAPTER 36

Contact Thwarted

_̴&_

We, like most of our neighbors, spent the next year in a trailer on the grounds of our damaged house as our home was being repaired. Our new normal included National Guardsmen patrolling local supermarkets. There were insurance adjusters blessed and cursed, contractors good and evil, workmen awful and wonderful, and cleanup, cleanup, cleanup.

Our beloved dog, Cleveland, died in November that year, 1992. I found her floating in the swimming pool one morning, like the guppies. My screams brought the family to me. As Mark scrambled in the water to get her out, our next-door neighbor Ken ran over and helped Mark pull her from the water and place her gently on the patio. After exchanging a glance with Mark, Ken knelt above her. He pushed on her chest and said, "Come on, Clevie."

Mark held Robin as I clutched Teddy, all of us weeping.

Ken put his mouth over Cleveland's muzzle and breathed into her, alternating with chest pushes. He used his fingers, not his hands, as one does for baby CPR. He worked for ten minutes before sitting back and mourning with us. Later, the veterinarian examined her body and told us Cleveland had had a heart attack first and then fallen in the pool. It was a small comfort that she hadn't drowned.

Through it all, I kept writing back and forth to Mikey's heart recipient family. We wrote each other about once a month. We weren't supposed to exchange identifying information, but over time a morsel slipped through. We learned the boy's first name: Nick. We let them know Mikey's name. I started signing my letters with my first name, and Nick's mother, Vicki, did the same.

We heard no complaints from the transplant coordinators who had warned us not to give out personal information. I wondered if the hospitals were still reading our letters.

One day, more than two years into the correspondence, I got a letter from Vicki with a different tone: "Haven't heard from you in a while; I hope all is okay. Everything good here."

I immediately wrote back, wondering if some disruption due to Hurricane Andrew had affected the way the local transplant team conveyed our letters. About six weeks later I got another letter from the heart-mother, as I thought of Vicki. "Still haven't heard from you. Have we offended you in some way? If you don't want to correspond anymore, that's okay, but please just let me know. We're worried."

I dashed off another letter and called our liaison at Jackson Hospital to inquire whether she had any idea why this was happening. She sidestepped any real answers and left me feeling uncomfortable, but I did as she suggested and waited yet again.

About four weeks later, two new letters arrived, one from Vicki and one from Nick. They were written in October 1992; I received them in mid-December. Reading Vicki's first, I could almost hear her tears.

"We have been so anxious to hear from you. It seems like ages since we heard from you. Is everything okay?"

She went on to report, "Nick is in the fifth grade. He is like a ray of sun on a rainy day. He is always happy and nothing ever gets him down…"

She closed her two-page letter, written in bright turquoise ink, with "Hopefully we will hear from you soon…May God bless you!"

"What is going on?" I wondered. Why wasn't she getting my letters? I read Nick's next.

> How are you? We hope we would get a letter from you. I sorta like school. I got all B's and A's on my gradecard. I also got—Nick talks and whispers too many times in class…Do you see snow? I love it to snow. I hope we get one foot. I make snowmen and angels in the snow. I will make Michael (angel). Gotta do homework. Write soon!
> Love, Nick

I held that precious letter in my hand. Then my neck got hot. Something was off. Something or someone was interfering. The thought crept up on me that my letters were being blocked.

I took a deep breath and pondered the topics of the last few letters we had successfully exchanged, now six or seven months ago. Innocuous stuff—spring is coming, her son is doing well, the grandparents celebrated a big anniversary. And something about God again. I found that letter and reread it.

> God needed a special angel in Heaven so he chose Mikey. Mikey sounds so much like Nick—there isn't a battle too big for them. I also feel God needed an angel on Earth so he chose Nick and together they are a team! God made them a team, and someday we will find out why, but right now I take comfort knowing that God chose Mikey and Nick…Nick says a prayer to Jesus every night before he goes to sleep to please bless the little angel in Heaven who shares his heart…

I remembered I responded to that letter with a more agnostic philosophy. I didn't denigrate her beliefs, but I made it clear that I didn't share them. Then I recalled a snippet of conversation I had with our hospital's liaison about a year earlier. She talked about her religious beliefs and how wonderful it must be to be a donor mother. I felt a stab in my own heart when she said that, but I let it go as well-meaning ignorance. She was young and childless and couldn't know.

My neck felt hot again. The letter I had written to Nick's mother was never sent to her. I felt sure. I was convinced I had been censored and censured, and I became incensed.

My response was to Vicki alone. It did not violate any of the stated rules for the correspondence. The heat in my neck spread to my face, and I realized I was gritting my teeth. I decided to act.

I was going to try to find Nick's family and write them directly. I began to plan my investigative attack.

CHAPTER 37

Searching for the Heart-Family

MARK AND I TALKED IT over and agreed we wanted to find and contact Vicki on our own. Mark's job as a news reporter and mine as a researcher gave us the tools to find things out.

We sat at the kitchen table with my favorite organizational implements: black coffee, a yellow legal pad, and freshly sharpened pencils.

"Okay," said Mark. "What do we already know?"

I said, "We know that Nick is about Mikey's age, and we're pretty sure he lives in Ohio."

Mark added, "We know he was critically ill and has a large family with grandparents, parents, and siblings."

I wrote all that on my legal pad under the heading "What We Know."

Between our coffee mugs, we spread out the letters from the recipient's family and read them again. Because of the hospital forwarding system, there were no postmarks.

Mark said, "Okay, we have what we know; now what can we surmise from these letters?"

I replied, "I get the feeling that they live in the country or maybe a small town."

"Yes," said Mark. "They mention the 4-H Club, and although cities have them too, there's something about the letters that make it seem that the people in this family are small-town or country people."

We moved the coffee mugs to the side and reread the letters, trying to feel our way into subtle clues that might be there.

"I think his siblings are older," said Mark. "It seems like he's the baby in the family, or at least he's the middle child. "

"Yes," I said. "I get that feeling too. And he was healthy before he needed a heart transplant. Vicki refers to sports activities he used to be involved in and is doing again. Remember that first letter he wrote us himself about the bikeathon?"

Mark said, "Ten miles!"

I replied, "What a terrific recovery he had. Oh, Mikey, what a heart."

A sob escaped me as I put the empty coffee mugs in the sink and brought out the wine. Mark stood up and hugged me. I leaned into him for a moment as I hugged him back. "No one else in the world besides you knows how I feel. What a god-awful thing to share."

"Yes," Mark replied. "Who knew that 'for better or worse' included this?"

I poured us each a glass of merlot.

"Back to work," I told him, smiling a little. We looked at the legal pad:

<u>What We Know</u>
Boy, Nick
Born 1981 or 1982
Previously healthy, sudden illness
Probably lives in Ohio
Religious, Christian
<u>What We're Guessing</u>
Lives in the country or small town
Older sibling(s)

We finished the wine, and Mark poured us each another. His hand shook a little, and he spilled a few drops of the merlot on the legal pad. While trying to wipe it up and in the process making a bigger mess, he said: "If Nick lives in a small town, there's a good chance the local media would be all over that story. I know I would—there can't be many seven- or eight-year-old boys to get heart transplants. The week it happened would be the most likely time for coverage. We've got to check the newspapers for that week."

But which newspapers should we check? One of the educators in the local transplant division had mentioned early on that the child had the surgery in Toledo. That didn't mean for certain that he lived in Ohio, as there weren't many hospitals doing heart transplants on children in 1990. He could have come from somewhere else in the Midwest, but Ohio was a strong possibility. We had done all we could that night. Mark and I toasted each other with the wine dregs and put the legal pad away.

"I'll go to the regional library after the kids go to school tomorrow," I told him, "and begin the research."

The next day saw me at a wooden table at the South Dade Regional Library. The library had been reopened for only a short time. Hurricane Andrew had done tremendous damage here. Resources were scant.

I managed to find a working microfiche machine. I asked the reference librarian for all Ohio newspapers for 1990. He crossed the room and came back with six little boxes.

"Here you are, the Ohio papers for the dates you wanted," he told me. "Do you know how to load them in the machine?"

He showed me, but it looked simpler than it was, at least for me. Threading the spools rarely went smoothly, and when one did go in easily it was likely to be upside down. After a while, I got better at it. Mark had advised me to check the dates from Mikey's death to a week later. He said from the journalist's point of view, this was the most likely time of coverage.

I watched the headlines zip by. The front pages from the *Cleveland Plain Dealer, Cincinnati Enquirer, Akron Beacon,* and *Columbus Dispatch* had similar information, mostly about world events. Although I couldn't help but glance at the front pages, my focus needed to be on the local pages, where the small-town events were most likely to be covered.

February 17
Front page: Contras' Campaign Tactics Could Boost Sandinistas
Local: Flooding, Tornadoes Strike across South Other Areas Are Hit by Ice, Snow Storms
February 18
Front page: AIDS-like Disease Linked to Monkeys
Local: Catching the Home and Garden Show
February 19
Front Page: Sharon Leaves Israeli Post, Challenges Shamir
Local: Grandview Seeking Help on '87 Homicide Case

February 20
Front Page: Cheney Visit Riles Filipinos; US Defense Commitment Restated
"Radical students pelted the American Embassy with rotten tomatoes and blew up a mailbox Monday to protest a visit by Defense Secretary Dick Cheney…"

At times, I fell into reading the stories. I had to remind myself to skim and move on. When it involved rotten tomatoes and Dick Cheney, though, the temptation was tough to resist. But I soldiered on.

Local: Another Big January for Area's Car Dealers
February 21
Front Page: Cuba Agrees to Resume Troop Pullout from Angola
Local: Site Near I-270 Called Best for New Bridge
February 22
Front Page: Exxon to Resume Oil-Spill Cleanup at Alaska Beaches
Local: Charges against Bar Owner Dismissed
February 23
Front Page: Greenspan Doubts Interest Rate Surge
Local: Heart Recipient out of Hospital

I stood up in excitement. This must be it. Still standing, I leaned over to peer into the viewer.

> Dayton Daily News (OH)—Feb. 23, 1990
> Ronald Herrmann turns 52 Saturday, but yesterday he received a gift he's been wanting for a long time. Herrmann left Ohio State University Hospitals. He had lived with an artificial Jarvik heart for more than a month before receiving a human heart early this month. Herrmann, known to family and friends as "Jack," will stay with relatives in the Columbus area before going home to Malta, Ohio, which is near McConnelsville....

I pulled back from the machine and sagged into the chair. My palms were damp. I sat a moment; then I mentally wished Mr. Herrmann well and moved on.

<u>February 24</u>
Front Page: Army Copter Crashes Kill 11 Soldiers in Panama
Local: House of Worship, a Profile of Columbus-Area Congregations

The machine whirred as it sped toward mid-February. I looked at my watch. I had another two hours before I had to pick up Teddy and Robin from school. I was still shaken from my disappointment. I looked back at the viewfinder and saw it had leaped into October during my moment of inattention. Back up, back up.

No, no, nothing here. I put the boxes I'd run through aside, worried I might be missing something. Maybe the newspaper that might have covered the story wasn't on this microfilm. Maybe the story was never covered at all. But I had to continue. This was all I had.

The next spool had a broken sprocket. I took it to the reference librarian who put tape on it. It went in the machine okay, but I was in for a bumpy ride as I turned the crank, advancing the dates.

February 17, 18, 19, 20, 21, 22, 23, 24. What if the story was covered but not until February 25?

"Stop it," I told myself. You've got the most likely dates—keep going. I took out the spool and put in one for the smaller Ohio papers. I focused and looked at the local headlines, starting again at the day Mikey died:

<u>February 17</u>
Brother Tim Leaving St. Vincent Hotel
<u>February 18</u>
Sinclair Student, 82, Finds Retirement Life Work of Art

I read on until the twenty-fourth and then rewound the spool and put it away. I looked over for the next box and saw there weren't any. I'd seen papers from Cleveland, Columbus, Akron, Cincinnati, Dayton, and more, but none from Toledo. I went back to the reference desk and waited while the woman in front of me had a long discussion with the librarian about Croatian artifacts she was researching. Finally it was my turn.

"Do you have any microfiche of newspapers from the Toledo, Ohio, area?" I asked the librarian.

"I'm not sure," he replied. "There's still a lot missing from the hurricane cleanup. We haven't reorganized everything yet. You're welcome to look in the box of unfiled microfiche if you want to plow through it."

"Yes, please!" I answered.

He took me to an adjacent conference room. Crates filled with boxes were piled along the wall. He pointed to one crate.

"These are mostly from Midwest newspapers. I think the dates you want might be there. Good luck."

I sat on the floor and began picking through the boxes. I organized little piles according to states. As I stacked the boxes, I thought of Mikey's initial frustration, and ultimate pride and pleasure, when his beloved therapist, Sissy, helped him learn to stack blocks. His cerebral palsy had made such fine motor skills difficult. But he'd persevered, and so would I.

After about ten minutes, I started finding Ohio boxes. I put them aside. There were three. Excited, I jumped up and ran back to the microfiche machine with the boxes clutched in my hand.

The first spool went in easily and sped along. The newspapers were out of Youngstown, Steubenville, and Sandusky. But nothing was from Toledo. I put in the second spool, and here, at last, were articles from the *Toledo Blade*. I looked at the local stories, and I glanced at my watch. I didn't have much time left before I had to leave the library to pick up Robin and Teddy.

<u>February 17</u>
Power Outages Worse Than '78
<u>February 18</u>
Optimism in '90 Farm Outlook
<u>February 19</u>
Boy, 7, Undergoes Heart Transplant

Stop. Tiptoe back. Another false alarm? But this is a child. He's the right age. It's got to be Nick. I felt the urge to stand up, but I didn't. I held my breath and read: "Nicholas Rohrs didn't get a new heart for Valentine's Day, but he has one now…"

I trembled, and my eyes closed. My shoulders felt cold. I put my tight fist to my mouth. Then I released my hand and put it back on the table. I opened my eyes and read it all.

I copied the name down carefully next to the wine stain on the yellow legal pad. Nick Rohrs. Nick Rohrs. My Mikey's heart lives on in a boy named Nick Rohrs.

Rohrs—my stomach flipped with a startle of recognition as I remembered my German vocabulary: das Rohr—a pipe or tube—a conduit of tears, flesh, and joy that connects us.

MONDAY, FEBRUARY 19, 1990

Boy, 7, undergoes heart transplant

BY JANET ROMAKER
BLADE STAFF WRITER

MALINTA, O. — Nicholas Rohrs didn't get a new heart for Valentine's Day, but he has one now.

The 7-year-old boy received the heart during a transplant operation that began at 9:30 p.m. Saturday and was completed at 3:30 a.m. yesterday, according to Jim Winkler, assistant director of communications at Medical College Hospital, Toledo, where Nicholas was listed in critical, but stable, condition this morning.

Nick is the 18th person — and the youngest — to receive a donated heart at the hospital. The only other child to receive a heart transplant at MCO was 10-year-old Ronald Turner in June, 1989.

Nick was placed on a computerized national organ donor list Feb. 4 and was classified as code 1, the most urgent need. Only 11 per cent of Nick's heart had been functioning after a virus attacked the child last month.

A second-grade pupil at Malinta, a Henry County community of about 350 residents, Nick has been in MCO for the last two weeks.

No information was given about the donor heart, except that the donor lived outside of the Toledo area, according to Kathleen Moriarty, transplant coordinator for Life Connection Of Northwestern Ohio.

The Malinta community has rallied around Nick and his family, offering financial and emotional support. Hearts United, a fund for contributions, has been set up at the Henry County Bank.

Nick's father, Larry, is a teacher at Four County Joint Vocational School, and his mother, Vicki, is a teacher's aide for handicapped students. They have declined media interviews, according to Mr. Winkler.

The town's reaction? A lot of happy hearts.

"The whole town is ecstatic. Everyone has heard the good news. The surgery went well. He's doing just fine. Everyone in the community is thanking God. It is so happy to hear good news," said JoLyn Nye, who has organized about 50 people in fund-raising efforts to help the family meet medical costs.

From 11 a.m. to 1:30 p.m. next Sunday, a fund-raising roast-beef dinner will be held at the Bavarian House in nearby Deshler. About 1,500 people are expected to attend the event.

"The benefit dinner was already planned for more fund-raising. This makes it quite the celebration," Mrs. Nye said about the transplant operation. "We are quite pleased."

Nicholas Rohrs

CHAPTER 38

Direct Contact

FROM THERE, IT WAS EASY.

It turned out that Larry, Nick's father, was a teacher. Vicki was a teacher's aide for disabled students. The research librarian who'd allowed me to go through the uncategorized boxes was delighted at my success.

"Thanks for stacking them in order," he told me as he helped me print out a copy of the story. There was a follow-up story on Nick's progress a few days later in the same newspaper. The librarian helped me print that one too.

I carefully put away the papers and my legal pad. I drove slowly to pick up Robin and Teddy from their schools. I barely noticed the familiar streets as I drove home with the kids, and I was distracted while they chatted in the backseat.

I called Mark when I got home, but he couldn't talk because he was about to go on the air. I called the telephone information service for the Rohrs' area. I wrote their phone number on the legal pad. I met Mark in the driveway when he got home that night. As he got out of the car, I shoved the printout of the article into his hand. He stood there, his briefcase in one hand, the article in another. He skimmed the paper and then read it again, more slowly. I watched his eyes move across the paper. When he got to the bottom for the second time, he looked up. Mark put his briefcase down and held me, with the paper still in his hand, against my back.

"Good job," he said. "You found him."

Mark shut the car door and looked at the microfiche printout, again.

"How bizarre," he said, his voice tight and high. "I'm glad you were successful but this…this brings us to a new level of reality. Mikey's heart is really in another boy's chest."

"We knew what happened, but seeing it as good news..." I stopped.

Mark's journalism training kicked in, and he said, "Well, it's got to be true if it's in the newspaper!"

We gave each other jittery smiles at the joke. Mark took a deep breath. In a more normal tone of voice, he asked, "Did you find their phone number?"

"Yes, but I've been waiting for you to get home before calling them," I told him.

We went in to the house together. Teddy and Robin ran to meet Mark, as usual, and he kissed and held them close for an extra moment. Teddy and Robin ran back to their rooms to finish their homework, and Mark and I went to the kitchen. Mark said I should be the one to call. I put my hand on Mark's chest, then turned away, and picked up the phone.

It rang only once—as if someone were waiting for me. A woman's cheery voice said, "Hello?"

I said, "Vicki Rohrs? Nick's mother?"

"Yes, indeed," she replied.

"This is Ronnie, Mikey's mother. Nick has Mikey's heart."

When I was about nine years old, I tumbled out of a tree I'd been climbing. I fell on my chest and stomach, and I remember the sound my breath made as it was slammed out of my lungs—a deep, hoarse "hhhuh." I remember wondering if I would ever breathe again. My lungs were empty—foreign and useless. It was an endless moment until they came alive again, and I could take in air once more.

That "hhhuh" was the sound I heard on the phone from the woman in Ohio. I kept silent and waited. I understood the silence, followed by a gasp.

"Oh, oh, oh, oh my God. How wonderful," she said, panting.

My voice cracked. "How is Nick? How are you?"

Behind me, I heard the rattle of ice cubes in a glass as Mark poured himself a Scotch.

"We're fine. He's great. Oh my. Are you all right? Why haven't you written? I'm so glad to hear from you. Where are you? How did you find us? Tell me all about Mikey."

I cried, she cried, Mark cried, and we talked nonstop for an hour.

CHAPTER 39

Learning More

After my phone call to Vicki, we kept in touch directly with the Rohrs family through letters, phone calls, birthday cards, and holiday gifts. We discovered Nick and I have the same birthday and that Vicki's birthday is the day Mikey died. The Rohrs and Londners each had three children in the same configuration: the eldest are girls (Robin and Amy), the middle children boys (Mikey and Nick), and the youngest also boys (Teddy and Matthew).

We invited each other to our homes but didn't visit. Mark was reluctant.

"Why?" I asked him, as I was eager to go.

"I don't know," he replied. "I think it would be too hard."

I didn't push Mark about meeting, but others did. Producers from Sally Jesse Raphael and Oprah Winfrey's television programs contacted us and invited the families to meet on their shows. I don't know how they found out about us; perhaps they saw an article in the Rohrs' local newspaper. I think they pictured a glorious cascade of tears as the Londners and Rohrs got face-to-face for the first time on their stage. Vicki and I had the same reaction: disgust. I felt a warmth for the woman who was as repelled as I was about being Schadenfreude entertainment. We did do one show together from our own homes via telephone—an Ohio radio station broadcast on organ donation. We also preached the gospel of organ donation separately. Mark and I did public service announcements for television; Nick's grandfather, Ken Fisher, stumped all over Ohio delivering more than one hundred talks on organ donation. He brought equally sized photos of the two boys to display.

I gave a talk on organ donation at the children's hospital where Mikey spent his first eighty days of life. My audience was physicians, nurses, hospital administrators, and families of donors and recipients. I told them I look upon organ donation as a beautiful rose grown on a pile of manure.

"You recent donor parents are likely still in the fire and searing pain of your grief," I explained. "My Mikey has died. As did your beloved child. That is our foul manure. But Nick is alive and flourishing. And so, I hope, are the recipients of your child's gift. Those are our roses. I'm glad something is growing, something beautiful."

Vicki and I were the main correspondents between our families, but Nick expressed his feelings strongly and creatively as well. In late 1994, at the age of twelve, he wrote a poem about Mikey. It still hangs in my house.

> Thanks to the Londner's
> for their kindness and love,
> They donated the organs of their child above.
>
> I will always love you for saving my life,
> I still can't imagine what you had to go through
> with all the pain and strife.
>
> You saved my life by giving me a Heart,
> So nothing will ever split us apart.
>
> I promise from the bottom
> of my heart,
> I won't forget Mikey~
> and what you did
> for me from the start.
> Love,
> Nick

Here was my response:

> Dearest Vicki, Larry, Nick, Matt, Amy, and Todd,
> I'm at a loss for words (a rare thing for me) about Nick's poem. We were crying before it was completely out of the package!
> It is beautiful, and you, Nick, are an amazing young man. I think most people in your position, especially kids, would try hard to forget where their heart came from. The fact that you love Mikey and continue to honor him makes us feel very glad. The poem and its beautiful frame have a place of honor in our family room.
> Thank you for remembering Mikey's birthday. We went to his grave and tried to imagine him at thirteen. Teddy went with Mark and me, but Robin waited in the car. She hates going. I don't force her.
> Robin got her driver's license yesterday! She's a good driver, but I'm nervous anyway because Miami has crazy drivers. Ted joined Cub Scouts—he is a Webelo. He looks adorable in his uniform, and he is so proud. He'll probably rejoin baseball this January.
> The weather is getting nice here—cooling off a bit. The high today is predicted to be only eighty-five degrees. Any chance you guys can come warm up this winter? You are welcome here anytime. Again, Nick, thank you more than words can say for your poem, "From the Heart." Nick, you are a very special, dear young man, and we love you. God bless you always.
> PS. Please tell Grandpa Ken I'll be writing him soon.

CHAPTER 40

Working Out My Grief

It was now four years since Mikey died. I was still overweight. I finally joined a gym. The membership entitled me to three free sessions with a personal trainer. I didn't think much of that. I thought personal trainers were an affectation of the wealthy. Who needs someone to count crunches for you?

Trainer Joe Neyra took my statistics that first day. My body fat was 26 percent and, at five feet tall, I weighed 141 pounds. Five minutes on the Stairmaster wore me out. I didn't know a barbell from a dumbbell or my gluteus maximus from my elbow.

Joe taught me, coached me, and encouraged me. By the third session, I was hooked. I signed up for ten more. The weight started coming off. Outside the gym, my mind felt stronger too. My work came easier. I cried less often.

A few times, especially during bicep curls, I'd cry in the gym. No one knew—at least, I don't think so. I'd wipe off my face as though I was just sweaty and get back to work.

Over the next year, I lost about fifteen pounds and weighed about 126 with a body fat percentage in the midteens. Two of my favorite exercises were the bench press and pull-ups. At first, my goal was to bench one hundred pounds. I was thrilled the day I made it. I jumped up and down on the rubber floor as Joe gave me a high five.

Once I passed the hundred-pound mark, I was eager for ever-higher one-repetition maximums. I did it the guy way: Before a new attempt my spotter would yell at me, "Come on, you shit," or something equally inspiring. He then would slap me in the face. While my cheeks were still stinging, I would throw my back onto the bench, feet flat on the floor, huff in and out a few times, grit my teeth, and push my arms up through the burden of weight into the arm lockout. When I would sit up afterward, I might be dizzy and feel a pull in my hamstrings.

The bench press is supposed to be a chest exercise, but it was a full body and soul exorcism for me.

I used anger and pain to help lift. Pain was better than misery, more understandable. My rage and grief went inside and powered me. It was fun; it was crazy. I eventually made it to a one-rep max of 170 pounds.

I loved squats and lunges too. What a great feeling to push up with my legs while my shoulders were weighed down. Sometimes I wasn't sure if I could complete that last rep—I'd teeter on the edge of collapse—and then I'd find another spark of strength and lock it out.

As my body learned to pick up heavier weights, my soul's heavy grief became easier to shoulder. While running in my neighborhood, I'd round a corner and come across a hedge of red and golden yellow hibiscus in full bloom. A nearby citrus tree would add its sweet scent, and my moment would slip into joy.

Many times, I was still overwhelmed and breathless with longing for Mikey. He came to me in dreams, and there I kissed him and held him with a frenzied intensity. I would wake up in tears, but by the time I dressed and got to the gym, I felt in control again.

I studied and became certified as a personal trainer with the American College of Sports Medicine. I took a further certification to work with people with chronic illnesses or disabilities. I believed that control or even partial control over their bodies would translate into other areas of their lives, as it did for me.

As my body got stronger and my mind cleared, I found it harder and harder to keep up with IVH Parents. The first question many people asked during our initial contact was why I formed the group. Did I have a child with IVH? How was he or she doing? When Mikey was alive, I could answer freely. But now I had to say, "He passed away."

I waited for the shocked silence that usually followed. Then, the braver souls asked, "Did it have anything to do with his IVH?"

I answered these frightened parents similarly to the way I answered Mikey's Montessori classmates: the doctors think he died because a weakened area in one of the brain's blood vessels burst. But although I tried to reassure parents that an aneurysm years later was unlikely, I just didn't know. It seems no one else did either; at least I could not find relevant studies. It's easy to find statistics on surviving the NICU and rates of disability among the survivors. But I found nothing on death years later relating to the initial IVH.

Over the years, many members, both parents and professionals, helped the group with time, money, or expertise. I hoped to pass the day-to-day duties, especially those first contacts with frightened parents, to one of them. But it never came to be. Finally, reluctantly, I gave up the group. I continued to get phone calls on my separate IVH Parents phone line for many years afterward, and I tried to help those who called. At last I realized I was keeping that phone line active because I didn't want people looking for the group to be disappointed. I had the line disconnected, feeling absurdly bereft.

Our direct contact with the Rohrs family, however, continued steadily and regularly over the next year. I felt a love and interest in the whole family, not only Nick.

When I opened our white mailbox at the end of the front walk and saw the big, friendly loops of Vicki's handwriting on the envelope, I felt a frisson of anticipation along with the ache of ongoing grief. She wrote "Miami, Fla.," not the more modern "FL." The stamps were always straight, and they often pictured something special like flowers or Elvis. As I walked in the house, I'd toss aside the bills from Southern Bell and Florida Power and Light, pile up the *New Yorker* and *Atlantic* magazines, and tear open Vicki's letters.

There was always a card and a handwritten letter inside it. The newsy letters told of Nick's baseball exploits, Amy's volleyball team, and the excitement when Matt won Ohio's honorable mention in football. Without fail, there was a grateful reference to Mikey and the heart the boys shared across time and distance.

Before our families had direct contact, Amy wrote her reflections. Later, she sent them to us. Her words gave us some insight into what Nick was like, before and three years after the transplant:

> My younger brother Nick was the most healthy, active child you can imagine. And, along with our brother Matt, mischievous. Once I came home from school to find my room completely toilet-papered. Another time I was taking a shower when a toad came flying over the top of the shower door. I didn't see my brothers but I sure heard them giggling.
>
> When Nick became ill at the age of seven, we just passed it off as the flu. The doctor thought the same and sent him home. When Nick still didn't get any better, my mom demanded tests. The next day, the doctor called and said to get Nick to a specialist in Toledo immediately. We were shocked to learn Nick's heart was functioning at only 11% of what it should have been and he needed a heart transplant to survive. We all went a little hysterical at this. Nick was more casual. He thought getting a new heart was like getting a new car—no big deal. The only thing Nick said was that he didn't want a dumb girl's heart—he wanted a boy's heart.
>
> He was classified first priority on the national waiting list. The days went by slowly, and it seemed like we waited forever. On my mom's birthday, February 17, we went to the hospital to throw a party for her. My mom got the best birthday gift she ever dreamed of—they just found Nick a heart.
>
> The surgery took six hours, and while we anxiously waited, I read some of the cards Nick received in the hospital. We stopped counting at 2,000. People were wonderful to us. Our tiny town of about 400 people got together and raised $50,000 to pay some of the medical costs.

At 5:00 a.m., the doctors came out and said Nick made it and was doing wonderfully. God was definitely answering our prayers.

He got stronger and stronger and two weeks after surgery he came home. Nick now has no restrictions other than daily medication. He is a perfectly normal child who plays football, goes swimming, plays basketball, and is up to his ornery tricks again. I don't seem to mind those tricks anymore because I'm just so grateful he's okay.

Nick was relieved to find out he did not get a girl's heart, although we did not know much more than that about the donor family. These people are truly gracious and generous. We feel very badly they had to lose a loved one in order for this miracle to happen, but maybe knowing they also saved a life helped heal some of their pain. They will never know how grateful we are.

Vicki's parents, Grandpa Ken and Grandma Rose, kept in touch as well. In 1994, Grandpa Ken, the family firecracker, published his book *Will Nick Ever Get to Be Eight?* It told the family's story. Mikey was featured prominently.

Nick's cardiologists examined him periodically and pronounced the heart "golden." The expected rate of heart ejection fraction, a measurement of the percentage of blood leaving the heart's left ventricle when it contracts, is 50 to 60 percent in a transplanted heart. Nick's radionuclide angiogram showed his initial rate at 55 and subsequent rates at 60 and on up to 70.

Nick played baseball, football, and basketball again. He did well in school, earning As and Bs. His career ambition was to be a doctor or nurse and help people get well.

CHAPTER 41

"Play Ball!"

Sports were important in our house too, especially to Mark. He played touch football with friends and softball on the Channel 7 team. He was good at ice hockey and even knocked the puck around with the Florida Panthers once for a news story. But like many a New York Jewish boy, his true passion was baseball. When we moved to Miami in 1978, the nearest professional baseball team was in Atlanta. A Mets fan for decades, Mark couldn't bring himself to root for the Braves.

Mark learned to love baseball in 1950s Brooklyn when he cheered with his father, Manny Londner, while they watched the Dodgers on a tiny black-and-white Philco television screen. Manny, a Holocaust survivor and immigrant like most of Mark's family, loved baseball and what it represented: to be an American. Mark was eager to pass that passion on to his children.

"Teddy, you're going to love it!" he said when rumors of a team in Florida began to surface. "Only one team for a whole state—sheesh. But better than nothing. In the city we had so many teams: the Giants, the Yankees, the Mets. And don't get me started on the Dodgers. My father never forgave them for moving—those bums," Mark said. He was referring to the infamous 1957 defection of the Brooklyn Dodgers to Los Angeles that was still lamented by many of our parents' generation.

So when the Marlins started playing in 1993, Mark immediately bought a Marlins cap and a share in season tickets. He wanted to distribute the baseball experience fairly, so the plan was for him to attend a game with Teddy, then a game with Robin, then a game with me, and then repeat starting with Teddy again. This arrangement lasted about two cycles, until Robin begged off her games.

"I'm so sorry, Pop," she said to Mark. "I know you love baseball, but I just can't get into it."

I kept going for a few more games. When Mark and I would get home, Teddy and Mark would spend the next hour analyzing and reliving plays Mark had seen in person and Teddy had watched on television.

"Can you believe it? A balk!"

"I know, a balk!"

Finally, I balked—I couldn't keep going to games when Ted was the one who should be sitting next to Mark at the stadium.

They became club-level fixtures, cheering, booing, and bonding as the Marlins won, lost, and persevered. If they didn't attend a game or watch it on television, Teddy would run out the next morning to pluck the *Miami Herald* from the front lawn so he could read the box scores aloud over his Cheerios.

In their fifth season, the Marlins became a wild card entry for the World Series, long shots to win. Mark met with the other families sharing in the season ticket purchase, and each family drew a World Series game to attend. When Mark drew game seven, there were "oohs" all around, as the game would either be exciting or nonexistent.

The Marlins took game one. Game two went to the Cleveland Indians. Game three, Marlins. Game four, Indians. Game five, Marlins. Game six, Indians.

Our season ticket group mates were jealous: Mark and Teddy were going to the seventh game of the World Series!

They each wore a Marlins hat and T-shirt. They left early for the game. I searched for them on TV whenever there were wide angles of the crowd at the stadium. So did Robin, who was watching with her friends at college. Neither of us could find Mark or Teddy. But we saw the game. We saw the Marlins go seven innings without scoring a run. We saw the Indians send in their closing pitcher at the bottom of the ninth. We saw the Marlins somehow rally to tie and then, finally, win the game in the eleventh inning and be presented with the World Series Trophy right there on the field.

Robin and I saw it, but Mark and Ted lived it. They were hoarse for days afterward, but they used their spent voices to discuss the game and its glory. Mark, with a little help from the Marlins, had sealed the deal: Teddy was a baseball fan for life.

CHAPTER 42

Sneaky Grandmother

As we prepared for Robin's college graduation from Florida State University in 1999, Mark's mother, Hanni, called Robin nearly every day.

"What do you think the weather will be like?"

"Where should we park the car at the arena where the graduation ceremony will be?"

"How many tickets will you get for graduation?"

Hanni would then call me and painstakingly relay each piece of what was, to her, exciting news. I would half-listen, smiling at Hanni's excitement at her first grandchild graduating from college, but not concerned about the unusually cold forecast or intricate parking instructions. However, I focused on Hanni's information the day she said Robin had only been able to secure five tickets to the actual graduation.

"But there are seven of us," I said, counting myself, Mark, Teddy, Hanni and her husband David, and my mother and father. That's what I said out loud. In my mind, the math was different: "Eight, there should be eight. Mikey should be a senior in high school, excited and proud of his big sister."

"The arena where the university holds the graduation is under construction this year," Hanni explained, with an insider's confidence born of her many phone calls to Robin. "Tickets have been harder than usual to get, and Robin was lucky to get five for the main area and two for the video room."

We decided David and my father would go to the video room. I knew neither of them would like that plan, but it seemed the most fair.

"Don't worry," Hanni said as we hung up, "it will work out."

On the drive to Tallahassee, Mark and I drove alone in a van we rented to load Robin's furniture from the apartment she shared with friends to bring back to our home. Teddy rode with my parents in their car, and Hanni and David brought up the rear in their car.

"I think it would be life affirming," I said to Mark. We were discussing—yet again—whether to meet the Rohrs. Robin's graduation made the passage of time acute. The next event on our family calendar should have been Michael's high school graduation.

"I think it would be depressing," Mark replied. "I'm happy for Nick's family. I want Nick to continue to grow into a strong man. I want to continue to hear about him and his family through Vicki's letters. I just don't want to see them."

"Why not?"

"Because I don't need to."

"But don't you want to?"

"Yes and no. But no."

The day of the graduation did turn out to be bitterly cold for Florida, and I envied Robin her extra layer of clothing as she zipped up her graduation gown outside the arena. She hugged each of us, careful not to dislodge her bobby-pinned mortarboard or her multicolored honor cords. She then disappeared inside the arena, lost amid gaggles of black-gown-clad soon-to-be-graduates.

"Let's go!" Hanni addressed our group, but she was already looking past us, bouncing onto her tiptoes to try to see into the arena. Inside, it was loud with chatter as people waited to enter the graduation. Mark doled out our group's five tickets to view the graduation in person and then the two tickets to see the ceremony on a television set. We five privileged ones handed our tickets to an official-looking person, who inspected them and then handed them back. We crossed a low partition into the main arena. Hanni then plucked Mark's returned ticket from his hand. She cupped it and her ticket in her palm. Hanni stood near the partition, her husband just on the other side. Hanni's palm went to her side, and the tickets seemed to disappear.

"What's going on?" I asked Mark a minute later as I watched the people waiting in line shuffle forward. "David and my father are coming through the partition to the main arena, not the video room."

Mark looked at his mother. Hanni grinned and nudged me.

"If they don't rip the tickets, they're still good, right?" she said. "I'm an old lady; I get confused."

I smiled at her, a little embarrassed but mostly proud. Mark and I each reached for one of her hands and squeezed it.

The seven of us made our way up the stairs to the graduation.

"If Mikey were here, I would be there," I thought, looking at the elevator.

When Robin's name was called and she walked across the stage, we all cheered. But Hanni's cheer was the loudest and the longest. When we reunited with Robin after the ceremony, Mark told her we had all been able to celebrate her bachelor's degree together and in person, thanks to Hanni's trick.

"How did Grandma think to do that?" the newly minted college graduate asked. "That's really smart!"

"Robin," Mark said, putting his hand on her shoulder, "this is a woman who survived the Holocaust. She spent years in a labor camp in Nazi Germany. She crossed numerous country lines during postwar chaos to get a ticket on a boat bound for America. She speaks five languages." Mark paused and took a breath. "She can sneak two grandfathers into a college graduation."

CHAPTER 43

Mark Beats the Odds

My enthusiasm for bodybuilding both inspired and annoyed Mark. He began running, somewhat begrudgingly at first, then with enthusiasm, and finally, with passion. Always meticulous, he wrote his times and distances on the whiteboard in the vestibule off the side door of the house. He was proud of his increasing distances, along with his shrinking running time and waistline. As a TV news reporter, Mark sometimes literally ran after his story. At five feet four inches, he was a short streak of lightening. Even the tallest cameramen had trouble keeping up with him—"Dammit, Mark, wait up!" called out the panting six-footers from behind.

One day, Mark commented that his times and distances were going in the wrong direction—slower and shorter than before. He seemed more tired too. He went to our family doctor in October 1999, to get a bump on his calf looked at. Dr. Taylor pronounced it a sebaceous cyst, but he sent it out to get analyzed. We were stunned to learn it was metastatic melanoma. By this time, Teddy was in high school and Robin had finished her bachelor's and master's degrees and was working in New York. We told the children what was happening, but we softened the medical news both for them and for ourselves. Mark and I refused to believe what his first oncologist had said: "The mortality rate for this is very high. You need to be prepared for the worst."

Mark had a wider excision of the tumor on his leg.

"Sorry," the surgeon said. "Your calf looks like dog meat, but it should be cancer-free."

Mark had chemotherapy and numerous tests. For eighteen months, there was no reoccurrence of cancer. As his leg healed, Mark went back to walking and then to running. We were able to forget his prognosis for days at a time. We let ourselves think it was over. Mark had surely beaten the odds.

Soon, Mark had more good news. In early 2001, it was announced that he had won the Silver Circle Award, an honor from the Suncoast Chapter of the National Academy of Television Arts and Sciences for people who have devoted a quarter of a century or more to the television industry. The ceremony would be in May.

Mark's unmatched intelligence, quickness, and memory served him well as a newsman. His employers prized his ability to take complicated concepts and explain them to viewers in an accurate, lively way. He was funny, erudite, and witty. In our family, if one of us said something particularly clever, we deemed it "Pop-worthy."

Mark asked Robin to look at the video and speech he prepared for the Silver Circle Award acceptance ceremony. He e-mailed her the video, and she watched it on her computer in Brooklyn.

"What did you think?" Mark asked her.

"I, um," she stammered. "I think it is very good, but it has a problem… in tone."

Mark didn't say anything.

Robin floundered for words, and they hung up. Five minutes later, Mark's phone rang.

"It sounds like a memorial," Robin explained.

"I know," Mark replied. We had high hopes the cancer would stay in remission, but Mark didn't change it.

That May, Robin flew down, and she, Teddy, and I accompanied Mark to receive his prize. My parents and Mark's mother and her husband met us at the swanky Mayfair Hotel in Coconut Grove. We sat together at a large, circular table. Mark and Teddy wore rented black tuxedoes. My father owned and wore his own tux—a powder-blue number with a matching, puffy bow tie. I thought all three of them looked fantastic.

Each honoree presented his or her video and then gave a speech.

Mark recalled, when he was a child, how his father would reprimand him when he sat too close to the television set.

"If you sit any closer to that thing, you'll fall into it," Manny Londner would scold.

The admonishment turned out to be a prophesy, and Mark expressed his gratitude to the people who helped him, personally and professionally. Local bigwigs then praised Mark as the best news writer they had ever seen and the best television reporter in town. Robin, Ted, and I grinned throughout. Mark gracefully and graciously accepted the accolades. He hefted the large plaque, grunting slightly with the effort. Then he put it down, and Robin grasped his arm as we huddled together and smiled at the waiting photographer for a family photo.

CHAPTER 44

Rushing to Robin

ROBIN WENT TO THE TWIN TOWERS occasionally, and when we couldn't get in touch with her for several hours on September 11, 2001, Mark and I were near frantic.

Mark left a message on Robin's voicemail at work. "I know you have no reason to go near the World Trade Center today," he said, willing it to be true. "But please call me."

My voicemail was similar: "Please call me. You know why. Just call." I knew the chances of her being in one of the Twin Towers was remote. But I also knew the reality of losing a child. My voice shook.

Robin called Mark at work first, knowing he would have to go on the air and needed to be assured of her safety. Next, she called me. When I finally heard her tight, teary voice, I trembled with relief.

"I just needed to know you are okay," I explained.

I thought of Mikey and how I had trusted Dr. Freund's diagnosis of an ear infection. I had figured everything would be fine, went to buy my son frozen yogurt, and then, hours later, was learning results of a cerebral blood flow study that proved my son's brain no longer functioned.

I needed to go to Robin, to hug her, to feel her hug in return.

There were no airplanes running, so I called my father and asked if he would drive with me from Miami to New York, a twenty-four-hour trip in a time of great fear. The Twin Towers were rubble, the Pentagon was a triangle, and there was a crater in a field in Pennsylvania. People were afraid to go to their cities' downtowns, and I was asking my father to drive up the Eastern Seaboard.

"What time do you want to leave?" he answered instantly.

Mark and Teddy stayed together at home while my folks and I packed the cavernous trunk of Daddy's Mercury Grand Marquis with food, clothes, and tools. We didn't know what we'd find, and my father believed in being prepared.

I chomped on hard sourdough pretzels through much of the Southern and mid-Atlantic states. It drove my father nuts.

"Can you please not crunch?" he asked plaintively, as we drove up I-95.

I tried gumming, but it wasn't the same. Thinking of the hours of exhausting driving my father was doing, I put the pretzel box in the backseat where I couldn't reach it.

Finally, after two days, we crossed from New Jersey to New York. We made it to the Goethals Bridge, fifteen miles from Robin's home in Brooklyn, where traffic congealed to a standstill. We sat there for five hours.

My father turned off the engine and opened the windows. We climbed out of the car and stretched our sore backs, looking over the bridge into the waters of the Arthur Kill strait. The bridge was full of other folks doing the same. On the right side of our car was an old-school, woody station wagon. We did an un–New York thing and made eye contact with the driver. She was climbing out from behind the wheel. She was a vibrant redhead wearing a fluorescent blue yarmulke. As we smiled at her, she began to speak, her Irish brogue completing the scenario.

"Hello, I hope you don't mind. I'm a diabetic, and it's been hours since I've eaten. I feel a bit wonky. Do you have any food you can spare?"

My mother quickly gathered a paper plate of grapes, cheese, and a chicken leg. My father reached for the pretzel box in the backseat, and then hesitated when he heard my pitiful protest. He put the brown box back on the floor, mumbling, "Too bad she isn't having a pretzel emergency."

It was evening when we finally crossed the bridge. The Twin Towers' stumps were smoldering, a ghostly red with black and gray plumes of smoke. When I embraced Robin at last, I finally satisfied my deep hunger to hold my daughter. As Robin hugged me back, I tried not think of the child I could never hold again. That first night, my parents, my daughter, a cat, and I all slept in Robin's tiny bed in the basement of the brownstone she shared with two other young women.

The next day we walked to Ground Zero, the name New Yorkers were using for the wreckage that had been the World Trade Center. There was an inch of dust on the ledges of the buildings nearby. I scooped some in my hand and put it in my pockets. Then, my shoulders shivered as I realized what I had handled: the ash of bricks, office furniture, papers, fuselage, airplane seats, fathers, mothers, children, babies, people, people, people.

I stopped in the street and took the dust out. People walked around me as I stared at the gray lump in my hand. I said *"Shema Yisrael Adonai Eloheinu Adonai Echad,"* the most basic Hebrew prayer and the one that came to me at that moment. I opened my fingers and let the dust go back to the dust.

We stayed about a week. Our good-byes to Robin were teary and long, but I had gotten the hugs I needed, and we had to get back home to Mark and Teddy. As I (quietly) ate pretzels while my father drove back down the Eastern Seaboard, my mother commented, "Thank goodness our Robin is safe. And now that Mark is stable, maybe we can relax."

"I'll try," I replied. "It doesn't come easy."

CHAPTER 45

Cancer Ablaze

MARK WAS DOING WELL. He went to work every day and to the oncologist every month. At each visit, the doctor looked at Mark's scan and told us the cancer was nowhere to be seen. Six visits later, the doctor pointed to the scan and said, "Here it is again."

Mark stared at me. I bit the inside of my cheek so hard I tasted blood. The doctor, sympathetic, recommended more chemo. We heard the words, went to the reception desk to make the appointment, and somehow shuffled out of the office.

This chemotherapy was different, harder than the first. We watched movies in the chemo room at the doctor's office. I tried to choose comedies. The first few days of chemo would be okay, but then the exhaustion would set in and Mark was bedridden for days. Then, when his energy returned, Mark went back to work.

Despite the therapy, the cancer spread. The doctor ordered procedures and surgeries, including the difficult Whipple operation. This operation involves the removal of the gallbladder, the head of the pancreas, the common bile duct, and parts of the duodenum and stomach.

Mark made a fierce and determined recovery from the eleven-hour surgery. He impressed the medical staff at Jackson Memorial Hospital as he painfully circled the halls, pulling his IV pole behind him. He had no tall cameramen trailing him this time, just nurses, doctors, and family in awe of his doggedness.

For a few months, Mark improved. Then an oncology scan came back with cancer ablaze.

"Your recovery is not very likely," the doctor said, looking at Mark. "I'm sorry."

I drove with one hand on the way home; the other was in Mark's. He was quiet.

When we got home, Mark went into the bathroom, stripped off his clothes, and stepped into the shower. I sat on our bed, listening to the water, unsure whether to stay in the bedroom or go to another part of the house to give Mark more privacy.

I heard a dull sound, then another one and another. I ran into the bathroom to see Mark punching the tile walls with the bottoms of his fists. He was sobbing—an angry cry.

"Mark?" I yelled to be heard over the water.

He turned off the shower and came out dripping wet. He pulled a towel from the rack.

"I'm going to miss so much," he said. "I'm going to miss seeing Robin and Teddy grow up. I'm going to miss grandchildren. You know I wanted to teach after I retire from WSVN."

I wanted to say something comforting, but the words dried up. Mark sat on the edge of our bed in his towel. I sat next to him, my head on his bare shoulder.

"And I'm worried about finances," he said. "We always were concerned about money for Mikey's needs, but now I'm concerned for you and Robin and Ted. How are you going to pay for Ted's college? I think about the mortgage, and hurricane insurance keeps going up."

I worked, but part-time, mostly from home so I could care for the children. Mark had been the major breadwinner for years.

"I don't want the loss of my income to be the loss of your way of life," he concluded.

"Try not to worry about the money," I said. "I can always get a full-time job. To help us both get a grip on this, why not go over the numbers with Daddy?"

Mark's face relaxed just a little. He nodded and got dressed.

In addition to my medical research work from home, I was working as a personal trainer at a gym and taking or teaching up to eleven classes a week in spinning and step aerobics. Teddy was a senior in high school, and he didn't want his classmates or teachers to know about Mark's health. He needed the escape of the ordinariness of high school. Robin was still working as a reporter at a trade journal in Manhattan. She called home every day to check on her father. Mark, despite his diagnosis and continued chemotherapy, needed the routine of work. He would talk by cell phone to Robin during their commutes, him driving in the car on US-1, her walking across the Brooklyn Bridge. Once at the office, though, Mark had new concerns.

"What will you want me to do if I lose my hair?" Mark had asked his boss, Alice Jacobs, when he first began chemotherapy.

"Mark," she said, locking eyes with him across her desk. "I'll put you on the air as long as you're comfortable going on the air. If you want to go on bald, I'll put you on bald."

Mark's hair did thin during chemo, but it remained thicker than most people's. Still, as his once-full frame grew gaunt, a viewer e-mailed Alice. The viewer identified himself as a nurse and wrote: "I can tell Mark Londner is ill, probably with cancer. Is there anything I can do to help? I would be discreet."

Alice printed out the e-mail and gave it to Mark, who brought it home. We stared at it, touched, but unsure what to do. Eventually, Mark replied, thanking the viewer for his concern but not commenting further.

My parents and Mark's mother were especially eager to see us on weekends. We would all gather, usually at my parents' house, and have lunch or dinner together. One afternoon, I noticed Mark and my father weren't in the living room with everyone else. I heard their voices through the wall. They were in my father's den with the door closed. I walked over and knocked.

"Come in, Ronnie-darling," my father said, his voice tight.

I opened the door and saw my father and husband sitting on the sofa. On a coffee table in front of them were papers and a yellow legal pad with columns of numbers. My dad had his hand on Mark's shoulder.

"What's this?" I asked.

My father looked at me while Mark looked at the papers and the yellow legal pad. "This," my father said, "is Mark being Mark."

He turned away from me and looked at Mark. "I remember the day Rita and I first met you. You knew you wanted to marry Ronnie, so you told us you had all your own teeth and you insisted on showing us your financial information. We trusted you then, and we trust you now."

I noticed then each man had a Scotch in front of him. These old-fashioned guys were adding up Mark's pension, his life insurance, and his projected Social Security payments. They were then subtracting our monthly expenses.

"I should be a part of this discussion. It was my idea to talk to my dad," I said.

"I know," Mark said. "I just needed to get it on paper with your dad first and then discuss it with you."

I kissed my husband and father and left the room. That evening, Mark showed me the legal pad. The numbers were all different financial scenarios. Across the bottom of the pad, under the numbers, Mark had written, "Hoping to live, preparing to die."

CHAPTER 46

Finding a Safe Space

~⸻~

THROUGHOUT THIS TIME, THE ROHRS wrote, called, and prayed for us. Nick got engaged, then married, to Ashley. Nick became a nurse. Ashley was a corrections officer in a local prison.

"Nick's grown up," I said to Mark after we both finished Vicki's latest cursive-script letter.

Mark nodded.

"We should meet him in person," I said. "His heart beats for Ashley now. We should meet her too." Mark paused and then said, "I just can't."

Meanwhile, Robin was a frequent flier between New York and Miami through much of 2001. In January 2002, her boss told her, "I want to talk to you, Robin."

Robin replied, "Good. I want to talk to you too."

The boss said, "Your work is great, and we are giving you a raise, retroactive to November. What did you want to tell me?"

Robin told him, "I quit. But thank you."

"I figured," the boss said and sighed. "You've been running back and forth to Miami to be with your father. I understand."

Robin came home shortly after and worked for the same company for a few months from her childhood bedroom. The Cabbage Patch Kids no longer perched on the top shelf of the closet, but Robin's reporter's notebooks and cell phone took up residence on the same desk where she had completed her multiplication homework. Then Robin got a local job that was barely local, commuting 110 miles round trip each day to a business journal in Deerfield

Beach. Mark's vision had deteriorated from chemotherapy side effects, and when Robin wasn't working or driving, she sat with her father, reading to him from *New Yorker* magazine articles, the daily newspapers, and all 432 pages of Paul Nagel's *John Quincy Adams: A Public Life, A Private Life*. They often held hands while she read.

Mark covered the big stories for thirty years, from the Miami race riots to presidential elections to Hurricane Andrew. In addition to his Silver Circle Award, he won eleven Emmys and the Peabody. He was the go-to guy on complicated stories. "Give it to Mark; he'll explain it to the viewers" was said by many a news director over the years. He made head-scratcher, gobbledygook material understandable, entertaining, and useful. He started out as an air force disk jockey while serving in Thailand during the Vietnam War. He called himself Captain America and played "subversive" music whenever he could sneak it in. He laughed like hell in recognition when he first saw Robin Williams in the movie *Good Morning, Vietnam*. He did it all—reporting, anchoring, writing, and editing. He was honest and accurate.

One of the many big stories he covered was the Challenger space shuttle explosion. He had extensive knowledge about the space program; he'd even signed up for the Journalist in Space program. Mark was a private pilot, and he drew diagrams for the nervous flyers in the family, like me, that proved how planes fly. When Challenger blew up on January 28, 1986, he told millions of South Florida viewers what was going on. That disaster was particularly poignant for us as my cousin by marriage, astronaut Judith Resnick, died in the explosion.

When space shuttle Columbia disintegrated over Texas on February 1, 2003, Mark had two rapt viewers: Robin and me.

Mark sat at the kitchen table in his cotton robe. He held a notepad and pencil. He'd been watching CNN. Reporters were asking questions, and he was writing down the answers. This was how he had processed disasters for decades. Sick as he was, he couldn't not report it. Mark crafted his notes into a story, which he read to Robin and me. He put forth the same effort for his audience of two that he would have for millions.

He was on antidepressants by then, but we weren't. When he finished and shuffled off back to the bedroom, Robin and I sat in the kitchen and wept.

Doris Stiles Glazer, the counselor with whom we talked after Mikey's birth and death, came to our home to help Mark deal with the pain and sorrow that fentanyl and lorazepam couldn't reach. She offered to make a guided meditation tape with him. Mark agreed.

She began by asking Mark to define his safe space.

"What do you mean?" he asked, lying in the bed with me next to him.

"For some people, it's the ocean," she explained, setting up the recorder and then sitting down at the foot of the bed. "For others it's a place in the woods. It's a place where, when you think of it, you feel peaceful and calm."

Mark thought.

"Can it be a person?" he asked. "Or a place on a person?"

Doris looked at him, unsure how to answer.

Mark reached for the front of my shoulder and patted it.

"This is my safe space," he said.

I couldn't speak. Being Mark's safe space was an honor.

"I've never had anyone choose a person before," Doris said. "I think it's a wonderful choice." She pressed "record" and began.

She spoke of tensing and releasing muscles. Her soothing voice reminded Mark that whenever he felt pain, physical or emotional, to go to his safe place and to relax and find peace there. At this point in the tape, Doris says: "Your head is on Ronnie's shoulder. You feel peaceful. You have no pain." Mark would listen to the tape, often falling asleep by the time the playback was done. When I was with him and his head was actually on my shoulder, I would listen to the hiss of the unrecorded part of the cassette as Mark slept. It gave me peace too.

Teddy came home for weekend visits from the University of Florida every few weeks during his first freshman semester in 2002. A bus picked Ted up not far from his dorm in Gainesville, drove for five hours, and then dropped him off at a shopping mall ten miles from our home in Miami.

Ted spent the winter holidays at home and then returned to school for his second semester. He followed his custom and visited home a few weeks later. That evening, after Mark went to sleep, Ted took me aside in the living room.

"Pop has lost a lot of weight, just since the Christmas break," he told me. Ted's hand was tugging at the back of his neck, and he was looking at the floor.

"Yes," I said. I told myself this wasn't like it was with Mikey. Teddy was eighteen years old, not six. He understood what was happening. I didn't need to tell Ted things he already knew.

"Okay," he said, still not looking at me.

The next day, Teddy took the bus back to his dorm. That evening, he called me crying. He understood what was happening. He wanted to come home. He wanted to be with Mark while he could.

But Mark himself was ambivalent with the idea of Teddy leaving school. "I don't want to disrupt Teddy's studies," Mark told me. "But I also don't want him to feel badly about not being here with us. I don't want him to look back and regret his choice, whatever it is."

Mark spoke from a similar, though not identical, personal experience. His own father had died during Mark's freshman year at college at the University of Missouri. After the funeral, Mark offered to quit school so he could help his mother run their small grocery store. She had insisted he go back to his studies, and he did. He often felt guilty over the years for returning to the relative comfort of college life in Columbia, Missouri, while his mother and younger brother held the store together back in Brooklyn. But Mark got something his mother prized more than her own comfort—a college education.

"It's not same situation. Teddy will go back to school," I pledged.

I didn't know how to get Teddy home, though. Robin and I were both caring for Mark. I called my father, my go-to guy and consistent hero. He quickly volunteered to pick Teddy up and to sign the required paperwork to suspend Teddy's university enrollment. He would also have to help Teddy pack and leave the dormitory. My father drove the Mercury Grand Marquis on its latest mission of mercy. A day later, it deposited a shaken Teddy with the items we had so recently purchased for his dorm room. Teddy, like his sister, moved back into his childhood bedroom and stayed home to be with Mark.

CHAPTER 47

Ethical Will

~~~

MARK REFUSED HOSPICE; HE PREFERRED to have only his family around him. He said we were his "safe place" in love and death.

There were a few times I wished we had the professional help of hospice. Once, Mark needed to be moved from one bed to another. The kids and I pushed the beds as close together as practical in preparation. Teddy and Robin each took a leg and I held Mark under his arms as his head rested against my stomach.

"On three, we pick Pop up and move him over, okay?" I told the kids. "One. Two. Three!"

In the no-man's-land between beds, I felt Mark slipping from my grasp. I saw my children's intense, loving faces as they held their father's legs. I looked down at my helpless husband and became enraged at our separate weaknesses. That rage gave me a surge of power, and I used my gym training to squat down, to push my stomach against Mark's shoulders to allow my hands to adjust my grip, and to put him safely on the bed. I trembled later with the retro-fear that I might have dropped him, causing him more pain.

Rabbi Rami came to visit Mark in his sickbed several times. Rami had the courage and tact to treat Mark the dying man as he had Mark the healthy man. Mark lay in bed, and I sat next to him. Mark and Rami spoke about the buildup to war in Iraq, the upcoming 2004 US presidential election, and other topical events. A former pacer himself who used to outrun folks a foot taller, Mark's eyes and head swiveled back and forth as Rami patrolled the tiled floor. Sometimes the discussions were deeply personal. Mark's voice was weak, and Rami waited without rushing him or anticipating his words.

During one visit, Mark revealed that one of the things he most hated about dying was not having any influence on the future.

"I asked my doctors if I could donate my organs, but the chemotherapy has ruined them for anyone else," Mark said. "Mikey lives on in Nick. How can I contribute even when I'm not here anymore?"

Rami stopped midstride and abruptly sat down in the wicker chair across from the bed. He looked down at the rug. Slowly, he raised his head and looked into Mark's eyes.

"Have you thought about making an ethical will?" he asked.

The ethical will is an ancient Jewish concept. It can be as simple as a short statement on a piece of notebook paper or as elaborate as a professionally produced DVD, but the object is the same: to document a person's wisdom, hopes, and dreams for future generations. Many ethical wills contain family history, personal stories, and life lessons. An ethical will can be an excellent tool to focus and articulate one of life's most important philosophical tasks: What impact have the world and I had on each other?

A testamentary will, Rami explained, is for distributing valuables. An ethical will, he said, is for expressing your values. Mark closed his eyes and reached across the bed quilt for my hand. He wasn't dozing; he was listening and concentrating through his morphine haze.

"What do you think about making an ethical will?" I asked Mark when Rami left later that afternoon.

"I want to do it," he said firmly, sounding stronger than he had for days. He pushed against the mattress and sat up. He had a goal. And a deadline.

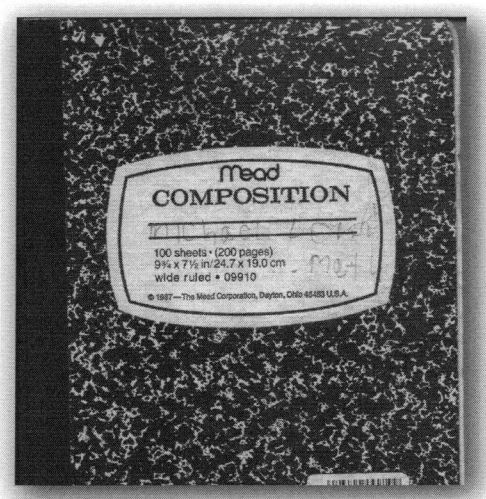

Mark's first step in creating his ethical will was to choose the materials. An undertaking this momentous shouldn't just be scrawled out with any old paper and pen. The intensity of such a task demanded old-school implements, not the laptop. One of my favorite short stories is *The New Engagement Book* by Jan Struthers. Mrs. Miniver, a middle-class housewife in 1940s wartime England, decides to purchase an engagement diary. Her initial choice is a dull-brown calf diary for the reasonable price of three shillings, nine pence. But, once out of the shop, she rushes back to exchange it for the one she really wanted in green lizard at the extravagant price of seven shillings, six pence. She recognizes the seemingly trivial objects we use every day are made momentous by their "terrible intimacy."

So when I explored the house for the right notebook for Mark's ethical will, I knew it was an important mission. I rejected legal pads, reporter's notebooks, and blank gift diaries. Then, in a pile of the children's old schoolbooks, I suddenly saw the perfect object. I clutched it to my chest and burst into tears. I ran with it to Mark, who lay dozing in our bed.

"What is it? Why are you crying?" he asked as my noisy entrance awakened him.

"Look," I said, showing him the black-and-white composition book I was holding. It was Mikey's last school notebook, started the week before he died. He'd written his name on the front, along with "Math." The first page had answers to some second-grade arithmetic problems in Mikey's wavering handwriting. The rest of the pages were blank.

"Shall we use this?" I asked Mark. He sobbed and put his hand out for it, nodding.

Mark's goal invigorated him. He got out of bed and leaned against me as I helped him put on his robe. But then he pulled away and stood alone. He knotted the tie firmly around his waist and slowly walked into the kitchen. I put Mikey's notebook and Mark's favorite gel pen on the table. Weak, and barely able to talk, he sat down and began to write.

I thought of the last time we sat here writing, intent on a vital goal. Then, we were trying to find Nick Rohrs. This time, Mark was finding himself, summarizing and analyzing his too-short life. But there was no merlot for the two of us now—just water and Ativan for one. Mark sat in his gray-striped cotton bathrobe, weak and gaunt, his protruding belly pregnant with death from the metastasized melanoma in his intestines. Just as he did life, he tackled this last task with thoughtfulness and integrity.

When he tired that day, he handed me the notebook, and we shuffled back to the bedroom. Over the next two days, I took his whispered dictation as he finished his message to the future. He was too weak to continue writing.

Once the ethical will was composed and edited, Mark gathered his strength again and recorded it from the bed as I held him and the microphone. Buoyed by his accomplishment, he decided to leave messages for our children.

For Robin, he recorded a message to be heard on her wedding day. She wasn't dating anyone at that time, but Mark knew the happy day would come, and he wanted to be part of it.

For Teddy, Mark left a message congratulating him on graduation from college. Ted was a freshman at the time, but Mark knew that happy day would come too. He wanted to do more.

"I want to make one for Rob's first baby, for all her babies. Teddy's wedding and babies too. That's the hardest, not being able to see them, hold them, teach them, and learn from them," he said.

But his strength was spent, and Mark could make no more.

CHAPTER 48

"Once in Love with Amy"

ROBIN AND I WERE SITTING at the kitchen table reading the newspapers one morning in late March 2003. Mark was in our bedroom, sleeping. During the last week or two, he'd been awake for shorter and shorter periods. I wasn't leaving home anymore for journeys longer than a walk to the mailbox in our front yard. I found the old baby monitor in the linen closet and installed it in the bedroom so I could move about the house and hear Mark breathe or call out.

The phone rang, and Robin picked it up. "Hi Suzi, how are you doing?"

I couldn't hear Suzi Doucha's reply, but Robin's eyes widened. "I'll get my mom," she told Suzi, and Robin thrust the phone at me.

I took the phone from her trembling hand.

"Suzi?" I said. "Are you okay?"

"Oh, Ronnie, Amy was killed in a car crash last night."

As a newspaper article in the *Gainesville Sun* described it the next day, an elderly driver sailed past a stop sign through the intersection of State Road 121 and County Road 326 in Levy County, Florida. He instantly ended the lives of Amy and her boyfriend, John, who were in John's pickup truck. Amy was a junior at the University of Florida, in Gainesville. John was attending nearby Santa Fe Community College. He and Amy were wearing their seat belts. Another young person, sixteen-year-old Henry Dyess, was also killed in the wreck.

When the two police officers came to the Douchas' door at 2:20 a.m. to report the accident, Suzi argued with them.

"She can't be dead," she told them over and over, standing barefoot in her nightgown in the open doorway. "We're going on vacation to Greece tomorrow; she can't be dead."

Roger burst into tears and held Suzi as she continued to berate the policemen. When the officers finally left, Suzi began the ghastly work of making it real. I was her third phone call.

When I finally hung up with Suzi, Robin and I cried our own grief. Amy was the little girl I'd nursed, who at six months of age gave me the gift of relactation while Suzi and I sang "Once in Love with Amy." Just yesterday, she was a blooming young woman. Brilliant, eager, committed to environmental and social issues, she had helped build a school in the Dominican Republic with her church and she had protested the new war in Iraq. Her boyfriend, John, was studying horticulture and planning to start a farm with Amy. This vital young couple was rolling along an open road, literally and figuratively, until a stranger's momentary inattention slammed their lives shut.

Robin and I briefly discussed and instantly agreed not to tell Mark during his periods of clarity. It would be too cruel and pointless. Roger was Mark's best friend. It would hurt Mark to know his friend was in pain. With Mark so ill, I realized I couldn't go to Amy's funeral if Mark was still alive.

CHAPTER 49

Ted's Gift

Just two days after Amy was killed, Robin and I heard Mark making unusual noises in his sleep. His lips moved, but no words came out, only sounds. His eyebrows and forehead were bunched, and his sunken cheeks seemed to move with each breath. It was four in the morning. Hanni had been sleeping in Robin's room, and I knocked on her door. She came to the door instantly, as if she had been waiting. She crossed the hall to be with her son. I then woke Ted, who had come home from the University of Florida to be with his father a few weeks earlier. Then I went back to Mark and Robin and now Hanni in my bedroom. As we women fluttered about Mark's bed, Ted, who had been in denial about his father's impending death, came in the room in his pajamas and messy hair and said, "Well, Pop, I guess this is it."

Ted kissed his father's cheek and began pacing about the room, talking about the baseball games they'd gone to together. Robin, Hanni, and I couldn't speak, so we touched Mark's hands and watched Teddy pace.

"Remember the ninety-seven World Series? It was you and me in those great seats behind first base for the seventh game. We ate all that junk food—hot dogs, ice cream, whatever we wanted—because it was the World Series. Then, the game went into extra innings. The bases were loaded in the bottom of the eleventh. Edgar Rentería singled a ground ball up the middle that hit off Nagy's glove. You started yelling, and you jumped up with your hands in the air. I didn't know what was happening, but Counsell was running home. He jumped on the plate. His fists went into the air, just like yours, Pop. Everyone was screaming. It was so loud. I was scared at first, but when

I saw you screaming and jumping up and down, I knew it was okay. I knew it was great! We won the World Series, Papa! We won and we were hugging each other and jumping up and down and it was the greatest thing, just the absolute greatest thing."

Mark, his eyes still shut, grinned. He was dying—and he was at the World Series. This time, Ted took Mark to the big game. Then Mark was out of the park. My beloved breathed no more. It was March 28, 2003. He was fifty-five years old.

CHAPTER 50

A Weekend of Funerals

~~~

MARK HAD DIED AS DAY broke. At the start of every newscast that Friday, WSVN played the video Mark had recorded for his Silver Circle Award. Robin, Ted, and I watched each one. Every time, the anchor introducing the video would cry. The noon news, the five o'clock news, the five thirty news, the six o'clock news, the six thirty news, and the ten o'clock news had marked our days for so many years. This day, we stopped each time to watch Mark's final report.

My parents and in-laws were at our house, and friends came by all day. Suzi and Roger Doucha didn't, though. They were planning Amy's funeral.

It was a weekend giddy with grief and eulogies.

On Saturday, Mari drove Robin, Teddy, and me to the church for Amy's service. We had to park a few blocks away because there was such a crowd. Amy had died six days before. Some friends sang "Seasons of Love" from the Broadway musical *Rent*. Another friend played a song on the guitar she had written about Amy after she died. Suzi stood in the wings of the church helping each performing friend wait his or her turn to honor Amy. Roger sat in the front row, his six-foot, four-inch body doubled over with wracking sobs. Robin, Teddy, and I sat behind him. We put our hands on his shoulders and on each other.

On Sunday, Rabbi Rami drove Robin, Teddy, and me to the cemetery for Mark's funeral. Rami sat in the driver's seat and, for a moment, I could close my eyes and pretend it was Mark driving us, as he had thousands of times before. "Mikey, Mark, Mikey, Mark," chanted my brain. I felt numb and nauseous.

When we arrived, a funeral home worker took Robin, Teddy, and me to an anteroom. My parents and in-laws soon joined us. There, we kissed, hugged, and shook hands with the family and friends who came to honor Mark. There were hundreds.

At Mark's service, Rami played the audio of the ethical will I helped Mark record a week earlier. For two minutes and fifty seconds, Mark's weak voice and strong words filled the silent, packed room. The words were meant for Robin and Teddy, but we allowed everyone to hear them and for WSVN to record them.

> An ethical will. To my children. Recorded March 20, 2003.
>
> I will always be with you. Even though we can no longer laugh or cry or embrace. I will always be with you in celebration and sorrow, in everyday triumph and disappointment.
>
> I'll be there, of course, only because you remember our beautiful years together. I wish I had lessons that would guarantee happiness and satisfaction in your lives, but I don't. I would ask you to follow these examples I considered important in my own life.
>
> One, guard your reputation. Your reputation for openness, honesty, and reliability is a treasure and will earn you the admiration of worthwhile people.
>
> Two, keep your Jewishness intact. It makes you more than a person. It makes you part of a great river we've talked about. It will be the source of self-respect throughout your years. And should you have children, their Jewishness will extend your being, just as yours has extended mine. At appropriate times, please say Kaddish for me.
>
> Three, never underestimate the power of love. It's something I thought I knew, but in my final days, I've come to learn the power of love as never before.
>
> Finally, try your best to enjoy fully all of life's treasures. When my father told me the world doesn't owe you a living, he was, strictly speaking, correct. But the world inevitably will give you beautiful things. Fill your senses and your heart with these things even as your

heart sometimes is broken by life's cruelties. All of this is advice I wish I had followed more closely in my own life. I offer it to you because you are extensions of my own life. And if you remember all of our time together, I will be there with you to see how you and life treat each other.

With limitless love,

Papa

Ed Ansin, the owner of WSVN, provided a lavish spread. People ate, laughed, and cried as they told Mark stories. Mark's coworkers told me they planned to take some of the words from the ethical will and engrave them on a plaque to hang in the newsroom.

At the end of Mark's funeral, Suzi Doucha and I slumped together in a doorway for a moment. As we embraced, I asked her, "So, whadduya doing next weekend?"

CHAPTER 51

Daddy

My darling father, Leonard Botwinick, stepped into the enormous breach Mark left behind and helped me with details of death and ongoing life. When I needed to learn how to fix things around the house, we went to Home Depot together, holding hands and squeezing them the way we had when I was a little girl. He helped me with the financial details of widowhood, drawing up budget after budget to ensure my financial security. I went to visit him and my mother often. One afternoon, about six months after Mark died, Robin and I walked in, and my father didn't run to the door with his usual greeting of "Ronnie-darling!" He was sitting in his den, and my mother led Robin and me in.

"I have something to tell you," he said.

Despite having quit smoking twenty-five years before, my father was diagnosed with lung cancer. The first oncologist said to give up, it was too late, and there was nothing to be done. Another doctor said removing a lobe of the lung could be the cure. My parents went with the second doctor.

The doctor ended up removing an entire lung, and then he ordered chemotherapy. I ran between their home an hour away in Broward County and the hospital on Miami Beach where the treatments and doctors were. Chemo, doctors, hospitals—the blur may have been from the crushing familiarity of it all or from my tears.

My mother and father were on their own in their house in Tamarac, and it tore me up to see their struggle. My father could barely speak, and my mother was working too hard, day and night. They had no help and little equipment to ease the difficulty of activities of daily life. To get to the toilet, for example, my father put his hands on my mother's shoulders for support, and she led the way as they shuffled together to the bathroom. The oncologist canceled the chemotherapy when it became apparent it had done no good. I wanted them to come home with me, but they repeatedly assured me that they were managing. I didn't buy it. It got harder and harder to leave their house. What if something happened in the night? One or both could easily fall. It would take me an hour to get to them, even flying up I-95 with my heart in my throat and my foot slammed on the gas pedal. I asked again, then begged, for them to come stay with me. They kept assuring me they were fine. I knew it wasn't so. Finally, I "kidnapped" my parents. I started packing two valises for them, and as I threw my mother's nightgowns and my father's slippers in the bags, they gave in.

"Okay, okay, we'll come for a bit," Daddy whispered. I could see the relief mixed with sadness on both their faces. But I felt that my high-handed tactics were right.

I settled my parents in my bedroom because the bathroom access was closest. As soon as I finished unpacking and put my father's slippers next to the bed, I asked him, "May I call hospice?" He nodded and squeezed my hand. Now my face showed the mixture of sorrow and relief.

Robin, Teddy, and I had cared for Mark when he was dying without the help of hospice. Mark did not want strangers in the house. It was heart- and back-wrenching. But the day after my father agreed, the hospice team of compassionate, competent nurses, doctors, and office people began helping all of us. Their care freed my mother, my kids, and me to just love Daddy, not having to strategize about how to move him or help with personal tasks. Teddy and I were working on a video for my mother's upcoming eightieth birthday, and we had the time to consult my father for details to make the surprise for my mother that much richer. We were rushing, hoping he would be able to view it with us. Meanwhile, my mother and Robin read to Daddy. We all laughed about the chocolate pudding and exploding whip cream at my fourteenth birthday party and retold other family stories. We bustled about the house. A few friends and relatives visited. One of the hospice nurses, Patricia, heard us telling golf stories. Daddy loved the game and always smiled when we talked about his good, bad, and ugly relationship with golf over the decades.

His voice nearly gone, he whispered, "I wish I could play one more time."

Patricia leaned over my father and said, "Maybe you can, Len. Let me see what I can do."

She got on the phone that afternoon and made arrangements: a special wheelchair for traversing from tee to green, oxygen equipment, and permission from a nearby course for all of us to go with him. Patricia, the blessed hospice nurse, reported her progress to us the next day. We had all gathered in the bedroom, and my father beamed as Patricia spoke. We knew he would likely be too weak to actually play, but he could be on the fairways and greens and could smile at the sand traps where he spent many an afternoon digging out. He had a future to look forward to. Planning that golf outing gave us all joy.

But the afternoon before we were scheduled to go, he fell into a sleep he didn't wake from. His face was relaxed as he slipped off, his hand in my mother's, his mouth in a soft smile. Although he and we did not have the satisfaction of the destination, we all had the sweet pleasure of the journey. I believe that my mother's eightieth birthday video and that last golf game, neither one completed, ran through his mind and eased his passing. He was surrounded by children and grandchildren, holding the hand of the woman he adored.

My father died one year and two months after Mark. Three of my four precious boys were gone.

At Daddy's funeral, I kept thinking about Coney Island. I had been a tiny child when Daddy and I went on the Coney Island Wonder Wheel, a giant Ferris wheel. It was just the two of us in the swinging gondola. The big wheel turned and we lifted into the Brooklyn sky. My father held my hand. We rocked a little as we climbed, and my little heart pounded as our world below grew smaller. How could this be? Why were things below shrinking, yet Daddy and I the same size? Why was the floor beneath me swaying? I didn't understand, and I was scared. Daddy looked at my face and took my hand.

"You know," Daddy said, giving my hand an extra squeeze, "I used to think about you when I was in the army."

"But I wasn't born yet," I said.

"But I loved you anyway," he said. "I had a feeling about you. When I was away from home, fighting in World War II, I would get lonely and scared sometimes. I made myself feel better by thinking about the happy times to come when the war was over and I had a wife and family. I especially thought about taking walks with my daughter—you!—and holding your hand."

I looked at my small hand in Daddy's large one. The gondola began to move.

Daddy said, "See, you were a little bit scared. But things are moving now and getting better, and we're still holding hands. I'll always hold your hand."

I lived a time before Michael, a time before Mark. But when time began for me, my father was already here. Like the air, the trees, the laws of physics, my father was here, before me, to guide me. Suddenly, he was not. The air and trees are still here, but my father is not.

At Daddy's funeral, I could feel his hand squeezing mine. He loved me before I was born. He loves me now.

CHAPTER 52

Messages from Mark

TWO YEARS AND THREE MONTHS after Mark died, Teddy graduated from the University of Florida.

After Ted walked across the stage and received his diploma, he, Robin, and I ran in the rain to the car so we could listen to Mark's voice through my car's tinny speakers. I put the CD in and pressed play. Mark had made this recording eight days before he died. The windshield wipers swished as Mark told Teddy, in part, "Congratulations on reaching another milestone in your life. I wish I could be there to share it with you. I shall have to anticipate this *naches* rather than being present to enjoy it firsthand. I can just see everyone bustling around in a flurry of kisses, pastries, and questions about what exactly you graduated in. You have always justified my confidence in you. Please imagine my huge hugs on this wonderful occasion. I love you tremendous."

A month later, we listened to the message Mark left Robin for when she got married. Robin and Jeff heard the wedding message a few days after they were pronounced man and wife. Robin hadn't wanted to hear it any earlier.

I had wanted Robin to listen to the message the day of her wedding. She had refused.

"It's too frightening," she explained. "What if what he says makes me so sad, I can't enjoy being a newlywed?"

Robin also said she knew this was the last recording her father had been able to make.

"I wanted to hear what he had to say," she explained. "Yet I also know this recording won't be my healthy father. It will be my sick father, a different guy, a more desperate guy."

The message wasn't for Robin alone; it also included her new husband. Jeff and Robin met five months after Mark died. Mark had made the recording for an imaginary bridegroom. Jeff's eyes widened, and he stood up from his chair almost as though Mark was in the room as we heard Mark say, "I am, however, consumed with curiosity about the lucky young man you are marrying. I am confident he has your wit and your integrity."

How fortunate we are that Mark was right.

Mark ended his wedding message by saying, "My wish for you is a life of trust, affection, and, of course, every kind of happiness. Love you tremendous, Papa."

CHAPTER 53

Disk Crash

AFTER A SUMMER AT HOME, Teddy began graduate school. Robin and Jeff lived about an hour away from me. I spoke with each of them, plus my mother, nearly every day on the phone. I needed to check in with my loved ones, just to make sure they were okay.

I got good at shoving at grief, slapping it back so I could function. I worked out at the gym. I was a griever who walked, pushed and pulled, lifted and ran, grunted and lunged. I climbed stairs, pedaled bicycles, and bench pressed ever-growing fractions of my weight. I was the physical metaphor of a mental block. Grief is heavy. I had to be strong. I still taught or took eleven gym classes a week and did personal training with clients before and after my day job as a medical researcher and writer.

In the evenings, I relaxed by taking a walk or light run. In February 2008, I was lacing up my running shoes when I noticed an ache in my butt on the side where Mikey used to ride on my hip. That spot had bothered me on and off for a few years, and I sometimes pushed my thumb hard into it to relieve the dull ache that came and went. But this was worse, more intense. I decided to forgo the jog and just walk. A half-block later, walking became problematic. I turned around and made my way home. I took a hot shower and went to bed.

The next morning when I tried to get out of bed, a shooting, stabbing pain threw me back against the mattress. I lay against the pillows, gasping. Anything more strenuous than shallow breathing caused electric pulses of pain from the right side of my butt down my right leg. I was in a smog of agony. Luckily, the telephone was at hand, and I called my mother and asked her to come over. I knew it would take her a while, as she lived an hour away and couldn't leave immediately. I didn't tell her how bad it was.

"Oh, God, I have to pee," I thought most of that day. I tried a few times to get up, but pain forced me back to immobility. Finally, I heard the key in the door as my mother let herself in at four o'clock, nearly eight hours from when I had called. She gasped when she saw my face, pinched and white with hurt. She began asking a flurry of questions, "What happened? How long have you been like this? Where is your ibuprofen?"

I'm afraid I was a bit brusque when I snapped back, "Oh, never mind any of that now—just help me get to the bathroom!"

Over the next few days, the searing pain eased enough for me to get to the doctor. I had a herniated disk, L2–L3, and bulging disks nearby. I saw many medical professionals during the following weeks, months, and eventually years. I tried a plethora of therapies including orthopedic, neurological, chiropractic, physical therapy, transcutaneous electrical nerve stimulation, yoga, bed rest, acupuncture, and energy healing.

I can't blame the therapies. The fault of my molasses-paced recovery lay within me. My emotions had me corkscrewed too tightly to allow the natural healing of my body. My usual coping strategy—movement—was gone. I felt my world shrink; I was pain-painted into a corner, hunched over and cringing.

The gym, where I'd spent so many hours, was wiped from my world. I had to cancel the classes I taught and the clients I trained. I left my school counseling job to take a full-time position directing medical research and writing at a company I'd worked part-time for years.

But the work, which I loved, was complicated by the physical pain that had rekindled my always smoldering grief.

"Sorrow can be so inconvenient," I said apologetically to a sympathetic workmate, who found me crying in the ladies' room one afternoon. I'd left a seminar abruptly when a speaker showed a graphic relating prematurity to brain injury in his PowerPoint presentation. The emotional punch took me unawares. I knew I had to get a grip on my emotions if I was going to be able to function in the world, especially now that I didn't have the physical outlet of running and weight lifting. I developed a variety of stress relievers that could be done covertly, and I was able to get through work and other public daily activities in greater comfort and control.

That is not to say I was without anxieties and fears. I had a repeating nightmare of falling down the shaft of a mine, a tin mine for some reason. I was in a tiny, narrow space and could see only the sides of the wall. My hands were pressed against the cold, clammy walls, and there was very little light. I couldn't stand and I couldn't sit. Within the dream, I craned my neck up to look for grass or trees—something familiar, green and alive. I'd jolt awake in a sweat and lie in bed, waiting for the first touches of pain. The meaning of the nightmare seemed straightforward enough: I didn't recognize my world, and I felt trapped, scared, and alone.

This time it wasn't another loved one gone from my life. It was my formerly able-bodied self. I had to make a new world, to be reborn. For that, I went to the waters.

I spent hours in the ocean, pool, or bath, where I felt soothed, buoyed, and freed. The beach was the best. I floated and rocked when the water was calm. I salted the ocean with tears for my beloved boys: my son, my husband, and my father. The hot sand I lay on molded to my back. The sun warmed me. I basked like a lizard.

As the weeks went by, I improved enough to get through the days in a tentative, guarded fashion. I looked back at my recent body builder glory and was jealous of my former self. Sitting brought on pain and tingling, so I paced the room during meetings at work, pausing to lean against walls.

I got a treadmill desk for my home office so I could walk while working. My understanding boss allowed me to do my job from home most days. A therapist helped me see how I'd set myself up for back injury years ago by carrying a seventy-pound child on my hip, throwing my skeleton off-balance and worsening a mild scoliosis. I had added to the problem by lifting heavy weights with an off-center base. In the gym's mirror, I'd seen that the barbells on my shoulders dipped to one side during squats, but all I did was add more weights and try to straighten up. I'd been told for years that I limped slightly, and I knew I looked like a twitching block of wood out on the dance floor.

"Your body whispers its displeasure first, and if you don't listen it will speak up louder and louder," the therapist told me.

But now I was listening to the roar of the disk. The pain had my full attention.

The therapist advised me, "If the body is overly tense, in chronic pain, or physically misaligned, it is virtually impossible for the mind to achieve a state of relaxation. You have been doing that for a long time. It is time to just be and to see what happens."

I resumed my walks at the park. It's about a mile from my house. It's free. After Hurricane Andrew, many of the park's old, glorious trees had fallen. Now, the new growth was finally tall enough to give shade. In my mine-shaft nightmare, I longed to see green and feel unobstructed. At the park, there are acres of grass and trees. In and along the canal that meanders through the park, there are white crested ducks, Egyptian geese, stately white ibis, squawking water hens and jumping fish. One time, when Teddy came home on a break from college, he and I saw a baby manatee. The frangipani trees rain pink blossoms several times a year.

I did gentle push-ups and triceps presses against a bench. I practiced down-stretching dog and sun-salutation asanas on the canal bank. I did a laid-back version of step aerobics on the cushioned surface of the playground. My pace was not frenetic as it had been in the gym. My heavy workouts got me through my grief over Mikey, Mark, and my father, but their intensity and pace hurt my body.

Nobody slapped me at the park, like they had when I was increasing my bench press weight. I no longer needed adrenaline bursts to move mountains of mourning. I started walking toward something, not fleeing.

Thinking about the future hurts, though, and it tangles with the past. I sometimes walk and wonder what Mikey would look like now, as a young adult. The answer is unknown, but there is some information that could help answer the question. It's like an algebraic equation—looking for x.

I play with solving the equation by looking at similar equations with all known factors. For example, I picture Teddy as a baby and as an eight-year-old. I fast-forward his sweet face until I arrive at Ted as the young adult he is now.

These factors are known: A (Ted as child) + t (time) = x (Ted now).

I do the same for Robin: B (Robin as child) + t (time) = x (Robin now).

So, I try to solve for "Mikey now," the variable. I picture Mikey the fragile baby, add Mikey the robust child, and attempt to solve for x, the unknown of Mikey now.

Dreaming past math to metaphysics, I try to visit an alternate universe through imaginings or meditation where Mikey exists with a complacent, oblivious me who never knew his death and only knew his growth.

CHAPTER 54

Meeting Nick, My Heart-Son

"My beloved son, Mikey, died twenty years ago. Today, I heard his heart beat again."

I wrote those words with a shaking hand as two tears slid down my cheeks onto the yellow legal pad I had brought with me from Miami. I was sitting in a modest hotel room in Napoleon, Ohio, after an astonishing day with Nick and his huge, loving family. I had allowed my desire to meet Nick to surface again. The Rohrs had extended numerous invitations over the years, but Mark had always felt too conflicted to go. But I felt a pull to be with the Rohrs, so when Vicki offered yet again, I accepted.

We arranged for the weekend of July 31–August 1, 2010. Teddy, nearly six when his brother died and now a young man of twenty-six, accompanied me. I could not have asked for a better companion. Robin wasn't able to come, as she had recently given birth to my first grandchild, Logan.

Ted and I flew to Cleveland and rented a car. I wondered what it would be like to be in a house where my son's heart still beat. Would the Rohrs family be uncomfortable around us? What would be the proper way to greet them? Ted and I drove two-and-a-half hours west. The grittiness turned grassy as the miles clicked along Interstate 80. I thought about that first night Mikey had slept in his bassinet at home and I had watched him breathe; about the night the ER doctor explained what it meant when Mikey didn't pass the doll's eye test. Mikey bouncing on my hip. Mikey practicing his Spanish. Mikey walking on crutches for the first time.

Ted took his eyes off the road for a moment and looked at me.

"Do you remember the toast parties, Mom?" he asked.

Jam-streaked knives in the sink. Mysterious crumbs. Inexplicably running out of bread. Teddy and Mikey giggling when their secret was revealed.

"I do; I do," I said. "But tell me the story anyway."

"The first secret I ever kept I shared with Mikey," Ted began. "Night after night, while the rest of you slept, he would direct me on midnight raids of the kitchen. It wasn't leftover meat or ice cream that we were after—it was toast: plain, simple toast."

"Why?" I asked.

"I don't remember," Ted said. "But I do remember that I took great pride in my role as the muscle of the operation. The procedure was simple: move the step stool to the freezer, climb, retrieve the bread, climb down; move the stool to the counter, climb, put the bread in the toaster, start it; wait a minute or two, stop the toaster since the timer never worked; retrieve the goods, climb down, make a getaway, and share the loot with the brains of the operation back at base."

From his smooth telling of the tale, I could tell that while my thoughts had been a jumble, Ted had been thinking intently about the toast parties.

"For how long did you two carry out this stealth toast operation?" I asked.

"Probably weeks," Ted said and shrugged. "Until an interloper blew the whole secret enterprise wide open."

"Robin," I recalled.

"There I was, just getting started on the step stool, retrieving the bread from the freezer. Then in walks my sister, bleary-eyed and looking utterly confused. I didn't hear her coming, and she startled me so much I'm lucky I didn't fall off the stool. I can see myself in the memory: wide-eyed, mouth open, white as a sheet with surprise," Ted said and paused.

"Then what?" I asked.

"That's where the memory stops," he said, his voice softening. "I don't recall what Robin asked me or what she asked Mikey or if she told you and Pop right then or if she waited until morning or if she yelled at me or anything else about the aftermath. For me, this story ends at the climax."

I reached out my hand and touched Ted's knuckles on the steering wheel.

"It's okay," he said and held my hand. "I'm happy to think about that old secret in its intact state, when it was just between Mikey and me."

We rode in silence for a while before taking an exit off the highway. I looked out the car window as the corn and soybean fields blurred by as Teddy drove down US 24. I smiled when I saw horses. When Teddy and I approached the Rohrs' house, I had no overwhelming expectations. Now, I was living in the present, not allowing the past to drown me or the future to intimidate me. We pulled into the driveway and sat in the car for a moment, looking at each other.

A woman opened the front door and trotted down the steps. "Ronnie? Teddy? Come in, welcome!" Vicki Rohrs, my counterpart, my counter-heart, embraced me.

I stepped over the threshold into an alternate universe. Here, February 17, 1990—the day Mikey died—was a day of joy.

Walking around the Rohrs' living room, I saw an odd juxtaposition of pictures of Mikey and Jesus. Not together, but next to each other.

Vicki took Ted and me into the backyard to meet Nick. Teddy clasped my damp hand as we stepped over another threshold. I felt my pulse quicken. There were lots of folks outside. Some people were sitting around a picnic table on the deck; others were tossing red and yellow bocce balls on the wide lawn that backed up into a cornfield. There were older folks, middle-agers, young people, and kids. There was a blond young woman with a smiling blond baby in her lap. She sat next to a young man with a shy smile. As Vicki steered me toward him, I was surprised to feel my heartbeat slow to a comfortable pace.

Teddy let go of my now dry and warm hand as Nick and I hugged awkwardly and looked at each other.

"Hey, Nick," I said. I touched his chest; I couldn't help it. He gave me a shy smile and didn't seem to mind at all that I—a stranger, yet closer to him than people he had known all his life—had put my hand on him.

"Hey," he said softly.

I could hear the murmur of the family and friends around us and the soft cackle of the dozen chickens in a nearby pen. I laughed as I thought how glad I was to meet Nick on his own turf, not in a Hollywood studio as Oprah and Sally Jessy had suggested.

I turned to Ashley, Nick's wife, and the cheery baby now standing in her lap.

"Hello, Micayla Grace," I said, smiling at my heart-granddaughter and reaching out to touch her soft cheek. Vicki had told me her name meant "thank you, Michael."

Teddy came forward, shook hands with Nick and Ashley, and admired Micayla.

Faces turned into family as we were introduced to Nick's father, Larry; sister, Amy; brother, Matt; Grandpa Ken; Grandma Rose; and the many children darting between the picnic table and the wide lawn. Joanne Walsh, who had been Nick's transplant coordinator in 1990, made the trip from Toledo just to meet us. Her involvement with the Rohrs became so intense that she married Nick's surgeon, and they named their own son Nick.

Vicki took my hand again and led me to a tree in the backyard.

"This is our Mikey tree," she told me. "It's a Rose of Sharron."

I laughed out loud—the tree was chock-full of purple blossoms. We have several "Mikey trees" at home in Miami, all Hong Kong Orchids. They, too, are full of purple flowers. We had planted one each year on the anniversary of Mikey's death until we ran out of places to plant them. I'd never mentioned to Vicki that purple was Mikey's favorite color, yet here it was. This Ohio tree to honor a Jewish boy had a small cross planted in the soil in front of it. But it was all love, and I was glad.

We spent the next several hours going in and out of the house, eating, drinking, and talking. Vicki and Amy set out a feast of baked chicken, salad, watermelon, corn, and cake. One of the chicken breasts was heart shaped. The cake, also heart shaped, said, "God Bless the Londners." It was awkward and touching.

The family firecracker—Vicki's father, Grandpa Ken—took me aside.

"I have five daughters. I tell each one she's the prettiest and she's my favorite," he told me, conspiratorially. "I feel like you're my daughter too. So I want you to know, Ronnie: you're the prettiest and you're my favorite."

I laughed, and we hugged.

My neck had been bare since I took off my teddy bear necklace the day Mikey died. Then, out on the deck of their house, Vicki Rohrs put a beautiful silver chain with a heart circling two hearts around my neck. This gift choked me up, but it didn't choke me. I breathed deeper and better as the extended Rohrs family encircled me with their love. I touched my throat and thought, "This necklace is staying on."

There was one thing I wanted I hadn't yet received. I had asked Vicki ahead of time, but I wanted to be sure it was still okay with Nick. He agreed, so I sat on the Rohrs' flowered sofa, stethoscope earpieces in my ears and my hand on Nick's knee. I listened and closed my eyes, memorizing the sound: thump-thump-thump-thump.

Mikey's heart, Nick's heart, their heart. And somehow, my heart, too.

EPILOGUE

Heart Sounds

~~~~~~

IT WAS 1981. I WAS pregnant with my second child, lying on the paper-covered vinyl examining table. My belly was jellied with conductive slime. My bladder was achingly full, as required by the procedure, so new it hadn't been common during my pregnancy with Robin. I winced when the doctor moved the wand around my abdomen. She searched among the placental whooshing sounds for the treasure of the heartbeat. Mark stood next to me, bending forward a little, staring at the screen, and listening eagerly. The images on the screen were murky to us, but the sounds were clear.

Whoosh-whoosh-whoosh-whoosh-whoosh-whoosh-whoosh-whoosh-thump-thump-whoosh-whoosh-whoosh-thump-thump-thump-thump-thump-thump...

"There it is," the doctor said. "Good and strong too. Sounds like your baby has an excellent heart."

Mark kept his eyes on the screen, but he reached back, groping for my hand. He squeezed it, hard.

"Ow!"

I laughed as he said, "Oh, that's tremendous!" He pointed to the screen and asked the doctor, "Is that the heart there?"

She answered in the affirmative as the glorious background music of a strong fetal heart thumped on.

Mark took a step back and held my hand softly this time. Our baby was real now that we heard the heart beating. My husband and I looked into each other's eyes, loving each other and our creation.

Mark whispered, "A new life. The possibilities are limitless. I wonder what impact our baby will have on the world?"

Sometimes I get a whiff of alignment, of Source, of that beautiful light and the bliss that follows. Every so often I feel what it's about, but other times it's more like a beautiful smell or sound that I don't recognize with my physical brain, but I know that I like it, that I *am* it. I look for peace—piece by piece. I stay in the darkness, allowing my soul's eyes to adjust to the new, softer light that is there. I lean into it, trying to go deeper, to find it, to identify it, to milk it, and to blend with it—but it's ephemeral. And then I remember, so am I. Then all at once, I'm there, and I can see. I'm home, and I'm happy.

Unstoppable Heart

*Michael Donald Londner age six
Summer of 1988*

*From left: Hope Ashton (born 12/07/2011),
Ashley, Nick, and Micayla Grace (born
11/10/09). Photo taken 2013.*

Acknowledgements

PATRICIA BLOOM. YOU WERE A wonderful boss at the University of Miami, and now a cherished friend and fellow author. Write on!

Todd Lazarus, Assistant Marketing Director, Columbia University Press. Your enthusiasm and excellent suggestions propelled me a long way. You are the godfather of this book.

Jennifer Crewe, President and Director at Columbia University Press. Thank you for your interest and support.

Felipe Azambuja. Your physical therapies and emotional support helped me learn to "be," not just "do." Kkkk!

Susie Sabean. Thank you for your heartfelt edits, lovely "sister"-in-Suzi-law.

Steven Ernst. Your suggestions and edits were insightful and instrumental in sharpening the book.

Alyson Grossman Traw. Your thorough reading and excellent suggestions took the book to the next level.

Alice Jacobs, WSVN Vice President of News, Miami and Boston. You lightened the load for the whole family with your support and appreciation of Mark.

Carmel Cafiero, WSVN Investigative Reporter. Dear friend to us all and Mark's colleague since 1973. He had enormous respect and fondness for you. I am grateful for your encouragement and support.

Jill Beach. Former WSVN anchor. I am so appreciative for your manuscript suggestions, encouragement and long friendship.

Roger Doucha and Robert Corbett. Just because —Three Musketeers.

Zhao Wen Steinhardt and Elaine Goncalves for their prodigious artistic talents.

Suzi Doucha: My bosom buddy (!) and sister-friend. You lived it all with me; I am grateful to you and for you beyond words.

Mari Salerno Fogel: My sister-friend and companion in mindful living. You, too, lived it all with me. You were a comfort to all of us in action, in speech and in silence.

Helen Harrison: Mentor, friend, supporter, and personal hero. Your pioneering works live on, but you are sorely missed. Onward.

Rita Steinhardt Botwinick: My splendid Mutti, the original *Sonnenschein*. Like the sun, you are bright, powerful and warming to all within your orbit.

Edward Hale Londner: In a profound, childhood way, you were closest to Mikey. What joy you gave him, being his brother. Your support and companionship when we met Nick and his family were vital. We listened to Mikey's heart again, together. How blessed am I that you are my son. I am grateful beyond all measure.

My deepest acknowledgement —
    Robin Joy Londner Rothberg: This book would have been a pale shadow of itself without your help, criticism, praise, suggestions, and occasional

benevolent brutality. You are a marvelous editor and writer. You were the propeller, the lion tamer and the midwife. How blessed am I that you are my daughter. I am grateful beyond all measure.

About the Author

Ronnie Botwinick Londner is a medical researcher and writer. She has coauthored several books on disability issues and written for many national and local publications on science and medical topics.

Londner teaches two popular courses at the University of Miami and other venues: *Helping Yourself or Others Through Life's Tragedies*, and *A Caregivers Guide: How to Do the Job Well While Preserving your Own Well-Being*.

The founder of two parent support groups, she has spoken at medical conferences, hospitals, and the University of Miami Medical School on ethics in neonatology, organ donation, parents' rights, and what physicians can do to avoid being sued.

In 1972, she was the first female motorcycle courier to work for a national television news network. She was thrilled when Walter Cronkite gave her the nickname, "Sparky."

Originally from Brooklyn, New York, Londner earned her master of education in counseling psychology from the University of Miami. The widow of a popular news reporter, Londner lives in Miami and has two surviving children and two grandsons.

Printed in Great Britain
by Amazon